P9-DUZ-230

ARNOLD SCHOENBERG

For Margot

Richard Fish

Arnold Schoenberg

ARNOLD SCHOENBERG

H. H. STUCKENSCHMIDT

Translated by
Edith Temple Roberts and Humphrey Searle

Riverside Community College
Li
4800 Mag   venue
Riverside,   92506

JOHN CALDER
LONDON

THIS TRANSLATION FIRST PUBLISHED
IN 1959 BY JOHN CALDER [PUBLISHERS] LTD.
17 SACKVILLE STREET, LONDON, W.1
ALL RIGHTS RESERVED
© COPYRIGHT JOHN CALDER [PUBLISHERS] LTD. 1959

ML410.S283 S92 1959
Stuckenschmidt, Hans Heinz,
1901-
Arnold Schoenberg.

PRINTED IN GREAT BRITAIN BY
THE DITCHLING PRESS, DITCHLING, HASSOCKS, SUSSEX

CONTENTS

ILLUSTRATIONS

TRANSLATOR'S PREFACE

H. H. STUCKENSCHMIDT, one of the leading musical figures in Germany today, was born at Strasbourg in 1901. During the 1920s he worked as a composer and music critic in Vienna, Paris, Berlin and Prague, returning in 1929 to Berlin, where he knew Schoenberg personally during the latter's last years in Europe. In 1937 Stuckenschmidt left Berlin because of his opposition to the Hitler régime and went to Prague: in 1941 he was compelled by the government to cease his critical activities, and in the following year he was called up for military service. In 1946 he was able to return to Berlin, where he quickly became one of the leaders of post-war German musical life. He was President of the German section of the International Society for Contemporary Music, and is Professor of Musical History at the Berlin Technical University, and also a member of the critical staff of the *Frankfurter Allgemeine Zeitung*. Apart from the present volume, he has published several books on modern music. In 1952 he was awarded the Schoenberg Medal for services to music.

This book on Schoenberg was originally published by the Atlantis Verlag, Zürich, in 1951, shortly before Schoenberg's death. This first edition was translated into French by Alexander von Spitzmuller and Claude Rostand, and was published by the Editions du Rocher, Monaco: the French edition was the first to contain the letter to the author from Thomas Mann which is prefaced to the book. In 1957 the Atlantis Verlag published a second German edition, which is considerably expanded from the first one, and it is from this second edition

9

that the present translation has been made. Apart from containing information about Schoenberg's last works, the second edition also has new sections on *Pierrot Lunaire*, *Kol Nidre*, the String Trio and several other works. However, as the author says in his preface to the second edition, this book does not attempt to present a complete account of Schoenberg's life and works, the proper evaluation of which must wait for a much larger volume: in the author's words, it is meant to be 'a guiding thread for those who seek a way to one of the most fascinating and enigmatic spirits of the century'.

As regards the translation of the technical terms, I have mainly used the same ones as in my translation of Josef Rufer's *Composition with Twelve Notes* (Rockliff, London 1954). I have however used 'row' for *Reihe* rather than 'series': the term *Grundgestalt*, which played such an important part in Herr Rufer's book, occurs much less frequently here, and I have normally translated it as 'basic idea' in the contexts in which it appears here.

H.S.

LETTER TO THE AUTHOR FROM THOMAS MANN

Pacific Palisades, Calif.
19 October 1951

Dear Herr Stuckenschmidt,

Many thanks for your letter and the gift of your fine book on Schoenberg, which would have helped me greatly if I had accepted Krenek's invitation to speak at the beginning of next year at the memorial service for Schoenberg. But I shall not dare to do so.

The opportunity of another personal meeting with Schoenberg, who had been ailing for some time, did not arise after all. Suffice it to say that I was absolutely determined not to increase his hostility, but to allow it to remain one-sided and never to say a bad word about him, and that this determination finally won the day. That I was so determined was sufficiently clear from my reply to his letter to the *Saturday Review of Literature*, and I reinforced my decision in a personal letter which I sent him, when somewhat later he published a very strange attack on myself in an English periodical—an article which the editors of the publication called 'a character document'. It did in fact document his character—as did all his pronouncements, which of course one cannot but reverence. To my letter he replied that I had made reconciliation, and that we should bury the hatchet. Yet he did not wish to perform this act in public, since those who had supported him in the 'Faustus' affair might be disappointed. Some special occasion, perhaps an eightieth birthday, might arise, where the peace treaty could be made public.

Alas, he did not live to see this. Before his death, though, another peace move took place: namely, when the *Saturday Review* wished to publish in an anthology the exchange of letters which had appeared there; I wrote to him at once that this was not my wish, and he, who had replied that his agreement would have to depend on mine, authorised me to inform the publishers that we were united in our refusal.

Once again, your book is very warm and beautiful and intelligent. I understand the New Music only very theoretically. Though I know something of it, I cannot really enjoy and love it. I have after all publicly explained that the triad-world of the 'Ring' is basically my musical home.

Yours sincerely,
THOMAS MANN

PREFACE TO THE SECOND EDITION

THE SUBJECT of this volume died shortly after its publication. The copy dedicated to him arrived on 14 July 1951, in Brentwood Park [Schoenberg's home in California: he died on 13 July 1951]. Since then the spiritual image of Schoenberg has not changed; but that of world music has. The influence which his personality exerted while he lived is now kept alive by his work alone. It has been proved that both those elements in his music which break new ground and those which create form have increased in power year by year. From the serial technique which was Schoenberg's creation, consequences have been drawn which also subordinate the rhythmic, dynamic and tone-colour elements of this music to a serial technique. All these things, however much they may have been developed in detail and made methodical by Alban Berg and Anton Webern, stem from the work of the Master. Two epoch-making events in the history of modern music are due to him. It was he who opened the gate to the land of music without key-feeling, and with it unveiled a world of new sounds, the comprehension of which brought the development of harmony to its end. It was he, too, who derived a comprehensive technique of composition from the historically developed law of twelve-note music, of which the first formulation was unquestionably that by Josef Mathias Hauer.

The most recent European school of composition which leans on Webern would neither exist nor be thinkable without Schoenberg's work. Athematic and pointillist music, organisation of tone-colour and rhythmic series have their roots in

Schoenberg. The possibility also of 'synthetic' music, as it exists today in electronic compositions, was considered by him in the 'twenties.

Above all, however, his style has become the essential element and characteristic of the newer music.

The conciliating force of time has softened many contrasts which had separated Schoenberg from some of his great contemporaries. Stravinsky's most recent development, through the inclusion and adoption of Schoenberg's technical methods, has once more brought about the unification of music: out of thesis and antithesis has come a fruitful synthesis.

Schoenberg had lived in a state of spiritual warfare with Thomas Mann, the author of *Doktor Faustus*, since 1947. Those who knew Schoenberg's way of life, his uncompromising attitude in artistic and spiritual matters, his defensive distrust of real and apparent opponents, also had to understand this rare and utterly regrettable discord.

I sent the first edition of this book in 1951, soon after Schoenberg's death, to Thomas Mann, with whom I had already spoken at length about the quarrel in 1949 in Hollywood. Mann's reply confirmed what I had hoped: that the hatchet had been buried. The poet authorised me to open my book with this reply just before the French edition was due to appear. So that this fine letter appeared first in a French translation. It appeared to me desirable also to open the German and English editions with it, since Thomas Mann attached value to the fact that the world should be authentically informed about this reconciliation.

Even with the additional matter in the second edition this book has become no more than was intended from the beginning: an attempt to sketch the life and spirit of Schoenberg. It will need many decades before the enormous mass of letters and documents can be fully utilised for an exhaustive biography. In the mean time this brief work may serve as a guiding thread for those who seek a way to one of the most fascinating and enigmatic spirits of the century.

Berlin-Dahlem, July 1957   H.H.S.

YOUTH AND ENVIRONMENT

THE MOST ORIGINAL and self-willed genius of recent musical history came from the Austrian petty bourgeoisie. Vienna, the capital on the periphery of central Europe, the residence of the Hapsburg Emperors and the crossroads of many cultures, represented the peak of industrial and commercial civilisation in the 1870s. Trade and commerce felt themselves secure in the consciousness of progress and scientifically guaranteed prosperity. Wars and crises seemed distant; from the victorious neighbouring state in the North and West a wave of a new spirit, which even the most solid traditions of the Austrians could not always resist, flowed toward the Danubian capital.

In the home of Arnold Schoenberg's parents little may have been felt of these signs of a new epoch: his father, Samuel Schoenberg, a middle-class businessman, and his mother, Pauline Nachod, did not belong to the grand world. They lived in modest, orderly circumstances and were able to give their children a middle-class education. Music played its traditional part in this, perhaps even a little more than that, for both parents loved and practised music. Among their children, two chose it as their profession—Heinrich Schoenberg, who was known as a bass singer at the German Opera in Prague, and Arnold. Born on 13 September 1874, he lost his father at the age of fifteen, while his mother, who was always in economic difficulties, had little time to look after his musical education. As a schoolboy he began to learn the violin in his eighth year. His first attempts at composition date from this time. Later he went over to the cello, in which, as in most of his achievements as a practical and theoretical musician, he was self-taught. With his schoolfellows he took part in chamber music, and the duets, trios and quartets which he composed at that time were written for this common music-making. We know little of his boyhood; but the controversies about contemporary poetry and painting then current in Vienna seem also to have found a lively echo among the circle of his friends. Interest in artistic matters was general among the youth of Vienna of the time, and the rich cultural life of the capital provided him with constant nourishment.

Schoenberg early became acquainted with the works of Wagner; he himself remarked to Dika Newlin that he had heard each one twenty to thirty times in his youth. In 1892, at the time of his sudden departure from the Realschule (grammar school), he was in the habit of strolling with like-minded contemporaries in loud discussion down the Haup-tallee of the Prater, and of listening to the music which a military band performed in the garden pavilion. At about this time he had become close to David Josef Bach, a friend of his youth. Bach described how Schoenberg met Alexander von Zemlinsky[1] in the orchestral society 'Polyhymnia', a union of students who were enthusiastic about music, and how Zem-linsky interested him in more serious musical studies. 'Poly-hymnia', which did not survive for long, can claim the credit of having given a prize to one of Schoenberg's works—the *Schilflied*, on a text of Nikolaus Lenau, of about 1895. D. J. Bach also stated that at this time Schoenberg, despite his fascina-tion by Wagner, was a confirmed Brahmsian, and communi-cated his enthusiasm for Brahms' chamber music to his circle. As a result of this meeting with Zemlinsky he was introduced into the 'Tonkuenstlerverein'. Brahms was associated with this, and the youth of Vienna harboured a shy reverence for him.

[1] Composer, 1872-1942.

The choice between Brahms and Wagner had already been a pressing spiritual problem for the generation before Schoenberg. Richard Strauss, ten years his senior, had begun as a Brahmsian of the strictest kind, only to change over to the New German School with all the radicalism of a renegade. In Vienna, where Eduard Hanslick defended the cause of Brahms in the Press, but where Bruckner also collected round himself a crowd of enthusiastic adherents of Wagner's music, discussion was particularly fervent. It is essential to read the reviews and memoirs of Hanslick to be able to understand the extent to which the question of Brahms or Wagner gripped not only musical circles, but also spilled over into social, journalistic, philosophical and political affairs. The possibility of any conciliation between the two warring camps, or even that of a creative synthesis, then seemed totally impossible. Zemlinsky, who had come from the strictest Viennese academic school, strove for this, more subconsciously than of deliberate purpose: but he was regarded by the Brahmsians as a follower of Wagner, as Hanslick proves in his review of his opera *Es war Einmal*.

Schoenberg's friendship with Zemlinsky, who was only two years older but was far more mature musically, developed rapidly. But in spite of the artistic encouragement which he received from his friend and mentor, he could not for the time being think of music as his profession. In 1891 Schoenberg entered a Viennese private bank as an employee in order to earn his living. This employment did not last for very long, and it satisfied his youthful spirit so little that it was a happy day for Schoenberg when his chief had to declare himself bankrupt in 1895. From then on his life was irrevocably dedicated to music. Among the musicians whose advice he sought was Richard Heuberger, the composer of the *Opernball*; he confirmed Schoenberg's gift as a composer and recom-

mended Schubert to him as a model. At this time he wrote a
string quartet in C major and some piano pieces influenced by
Brahms. Zemlinsky, with whom Schoenberg worked for
several months on counterpoint, also led him towards practical
activities, and so in 1895 he took over the conductorship of the
metal workers' choral society in Stockerau near Vienna.
With his worker-singers Schoenberg even attempted Brahms'
choruses, although his lack of knowledge of piano-playing
made rehearsals more difficult.

Egon Wellesz in his biography, which appeared in 1921,
mentions the intellectual circle of the Landtmann and Grien-
steidl Cafés which Schoenberg frequented and where he took
part in lively discussions about Wagner's *Tristan*. It is significant for the spiritual independence of the young musician that
in spite of moving in such decidedly Wagnerian circles his
position as a composer remained uninfluenced. In the summer
of 1897 he made the piano score of Zemlinsky's opera *Sarema*
and also wrote a string quartet in D major, which had its first
performance during the next season, when it was played by
the Fitzner Quartet in Vienna and aroused attention. This was
the time, too, when he composed several of the Lieder which
were published later as Opus 1-3 by the Berlin Dreililienverlag:
these may be regarded as Schoenberg's first mature compositions.

Life was not encouraging for Schoenberg at this time. For
years he fought against material poverty, with which the
income from Stockerau could help only in part. Thus he was
forced to take on musical work which was utterly foreign to
his spiritual constitution. From 1900 onwards he scored song
hits and operettas—an activity which prevented for years the
completion of large works, in particular the *Gurrelieder* which
he had begun at the turn of the century. Simultaneously he
thought of marriage: the sister of his friend, Mathilde von

Zemlinsky, became engaged to him and on 7 October 1901 became his wife. Shortly after their marriage, in December of that year, the couple left Vienna. Schoenberg had been engaged as conductor at Ernst von Wolzogen's 'Ueberbrettl' at the Berlin Bunte Theater. It seems like an irony of fate that the musician of his time least likely to compromise, the man who would rather do without a public than make the slightest concession to the taste of the masses, had to spend his time scoring and conducting light music. Yet the 'Ueberbrettl' had literary ambitions, and Schoenberg himself contributed to the repertory a song with trumpet obbligato: it had to be dropped after the first performance. The contact with the Wolzogen circle played little part in his artistic development, unless one regards Albert Giraud's *Pierrot Lunaire* poems and their German translation by Otto Erich Hartleben, which Schoenberg used ten years later for one of his most important works, as part of the spirit of the 'Ueberbrettl'.

Among the manuscripts which travelled to Berlin with him was the uncompleted score of the mighty choral work the *Gurrelieder*, on poems of Jens Peter Jacobsen;[1] this was begun in February 1900 and finally completed in short score in May 1901. Richard Strauss was much interested in the work, the instrumentation of which Schoenberg had to interrupt in favour of scoring operettas (and it was only completed in 1911). Strauss, who was already famous and influential then, helped him to gain the Liszt scholarship—the income of the Liszt foundation which was annually given by the Allgemeine Deutsche Musikverein to a gifted composer or pianist. At the same time he recommended Schoenberg as a teacher of composition to the Stern Conservatoire. This was an activity more to his liking than that of a cabaret conductor, from which he soon resigned. But Berlin at this time could not hold him

[1] Danish poet who lived in the second half of the nineteenth century.

for long. In July 1903 he returned to Vienna. In the twenty months spent in Berlin the only large work completed was the symphonic poem *Pelleas und Melisande*. He had been stimulated to undertake it by Richard Strauss, who suggested to Schoenberg Maurice Maeterlinck's drama as a possible operatic libretto—in the same year as the first performance of Debussy's opera in Paris. Schoenberg's eldest daughter, Trudi, was born in 1902. She later married the composer Felix Greissle and died in New York in 1947.

THE SPIRIT OF THE EARLY WORKS

ALREADY in the early songs opus 1-3, the string sextet *Verklaerte Nacht*, the *Gurrelieder* and the tone poem *Pelleas und Melisande* Schoenberg showed himself to be a musician of the progressive school and even of the avant-garde. But he did not stand alone; his works, on the surface at least, hardly fall outside the framework of what was being written in Europe at about that time. Already in 1895 Richard Strauss had stirred up the minds of the conservatives with *Till Eulenspiegel*, and he had continued his 'New German' boldnesses in *Heldenleben*, the *Sinfonia Domestica* and the comic opera *Feuersnot*. Alexander Skriabin was in the process of conquering a realm of mystic hyper-romanticism derived from the world of Chopin. With his three Nocturnes and in his *Pelleas*, Debussy had opened up new regions of sound and of functionless harmony. Gustav Mahler's 4th symphony, and the first Lieder and organ works of Max Reger, enlarged the possibilities of polyphonic writing through richer chromatic harmony. The operas of Puccini, above all *Tosca*, were enriching the harmonic and melodic vocabulary of music.

Schoenberg knew little of these works, with the exception of the scores of Strauss. He arrived at similar results independently, and because of his own personal radicalism he emphasised them more strongly than his contemporaries did. He found his texts among the lyricists of the German naturalistic school, who also often inspired Strauss; they included poets such as Richard Dehmel and Johannes Schlaf. Even the sextet is based on a poem by Dehmel. At the first performance of the first

Lieder in 1898 there was a small uproar in the hall; 'and it has never ceased since', as Schoenberg said with a smile to his pupil René Leibowitz, the head of the Paris school of twelve-note composers. Two lieder by Dehmel in Opus 2 indicate the trend towards later developments. The first, *Erwartung*, contains the often quoted chords, which through the fanwise

chromatic movement of four notes reach a five-part E flat major chord and anticipate the 'fourths' of Debussy and Skriabin and also combinations of chords in Strauss's *Salome* and *Elektra*. In the second song, *Schenk mir deinen goldnen Kamm*, the principle of interpreting every note of a chord as a possible leading-note upwards and downwards has been carried through to result in the complete obscuring of the tonality. The all-pervading presence of the chromatic scale is already effective as an unconscious law here.

All these harmonic changes can of course be traced back to the chromaticism of *Tristan;* they are the logical results of romantic harmony, and are examples for the stylistic examinations of Ernst Kurth.[1] And, as in the late works of Wagner, a new polyphonic feeling develops here out of the impulse for progressive alteration; this allocates a function of decisive importance to the middle parts. Even though this music is

[1] Viennese musicologist and theoretician, 1886-1946.

conceived entirely on the basis of sound, it lacks the flatness of homophony; its effect is altogether three-dimensional, for its texture is thought out and developed contrapuntally. In harmonic expression of a high romantic richness, which is often extravagant in its character and in the art of interpreting words and meaning, it shows in its structure an organic whole, a sense of direction of development, a pleasure in variation and motivic development, which would be unthinkable without Brahms' influence. It is as it were dramatic chamber music, an *espressivo* achieved by the cleanest means and also the most imaginative thematic working. The classic Viennese principle of Beethoven's 'obbligato accompaniment' is here used in the service of an unusually expansive will for expression which does not shy before any kind of novelty.

Although in these songs and in those of opus 3 harmony and polyphonic movement are of the highest importance, their immediate effect springs from the special kind of melody which characterises them. Schoenberg's melodic invention remained unchanged in its character from his first works to his last. It is the true substance of his music and of its invention. Its wealth of expression, its exaltation and its pregnancy go beyond anything that has been attempted in the sphere of post-romantic music. In the Lieder, to whose text and sentiments it corresponds with aesthetic completeness, it leads a complete life of its own, which is never surrendered in favour of illustrative elements. And like everything that is alive, it is difficult to analyse; in spite of its unmistakable characteristics, it is impossible to examine it systematically. Certainly some typical turns of phrase can be established: the emphasis on notes foreign to the harmony, the preference for large intervals and the tensions that go with this, the chromatic colouring, the free rhythm which is almost independent of the bar line, the avoidance of sequences and pedantic repetitions, the preference for varied repetitions and above all for motivic variation. In general—and this differentiates it in principle from that of Wagner—Schoenberg's melody avoids the use of broken triads; its usual form is the change between diatonic or chromatic steps and leaps of octaves, sixths or sevenths. From this type of melody, there results an 'espressivo-character' with its corresponding dynamics and phrasing, which demands a special style of performance for all of Schoenberg's music.

The sextet *Verklaerte Nacht* shows all these characteristics of harmony, counterpoint and melody with the enlargements and modifications which result from the extraordinary breadth of form in this work. Like almost all of Schoenberg's compositions, it was written in a brief space of time—in three weeks in September 1899, during a holiday in the country. For its programmatic basis it takes a poem from Dehmel's novel *Zwei Menschen*, whose sombre basic note and emotion—a mixture of romanticism and naturalism—are reproduced in the music and also heightened in expression. The form, corresponding to 'New German' examples (Liszt's B minor sonata), is free and in one movement; the numerous themes are developed according to the poetic material, without achieving more definite symphonic forms or regular development. All is here directed towards expression, melodic and polyphonic flow and romantic excitement. The pathos of an erotic experience shared by two people, strengthened by a highly sensitive exploration of new realms of sound, here acquires a subjective form throughout. The audience of this piece at the first performance, given by Arnold Rosé in the Vienna Tonkuenstlerverein in 1903, was shocked; people were as offended by some of Schoenberg's forbidden chords as by the transfer of programme music into the field of chamber music. In fact this music at the time was as incomprehensible and alarming as the first twelve-note compositions of Schoenberg twenty years later. The public today regards it as romantic and emotional.

With his sextet Schoenberg had tried his strength in a large form: he now felt up to the largest task which he was ever to face. The *Gurrelieder* in both text and instrumentation is a true post-Wagnerian work, completely dramatic in effect. Composed in 1900 (but the instrumentation took until 1911), it is comparable in breadth of conception and execution with the giant symphonies of Gustav Mahler and in musical language perhaps with the symphonic poems of Richard Strauss and the early music dramas of Hans Pfitzner. It is written for five solo voices (soprano, mezzo-soprano, two tenors and bass), one speaking voice, three four-part male choruses and an eight-part mixed chorus, and an orchestra which includes four flutes and four piccolos, three oboes, two English horns, three clarinets in A or B flat, two E flat clarinets, two bass clarinets, three bassoons, two contra-bassoons, ten horns in F, six trumpets, one bass trumpet, seven trombones, one bass trombone, one contrabass tuba, six timpani, numerous percussion instruments, four harps, celesta and strings (violins in ten parts and violas and cellos divided into eight parts each).

The three parts of the work, which lasts two hours, can be likened to song forms, linked by interludes. Jacobsen's poems, which are expressive and particularly beautiful in language, describe the love of a King Waldemar for Tove, his despairing pain when the loved one dies, the *Wilde Jagd* (wild hunt)—the departure of Waldemar's dead men—and the transfiguring end with its idea of resurrection. In the frequent changes between solo song, chorus, speaking over music and illustrative orchestral passages a highly dramatic and lyrical language is given expression and an extraordinary range of different moods is developed. The rich diatonic harmony, chromatically embellished and with a tendency to colour the major chords with the sensual added sixth, would be unthinkable without

Wagner's example. The melodic line, however, shows the typically Schoenbergian stamp of wide intervals, and the polyphony in the choral and orchestral passages goes well beyond the bounds of late romantic music. For the first time Schoenberg here (in the third part of the *Gurrelieder*, before the final chorus) links music and the spoken word, an idea which he later returned to in the music drama *Die Glueckliche Hand*, and which dominates *Pierrot Lunaire*; it also makes a sporadic appearance in the light opera *Von heute auf morgen*, and finally is dominant in three works of his final creative period: *Kol Nidre*, the *Ode to Napoleon* and the *Survivor from Warsaw*. The unusually large size of the orchestra serves less to make massive sound effects (though the score is not devoid of these) than to make it possible to score chords or sections in a unified tone-colour. The deep earnestness of the work, its fantastic melodiousness and colour, its link with mythical figures, all make it worth while to try and overcome the difficulties of performance. Since its first performance by the Vienna Philharmonic Chorus under Franz Schreker[1] on 23 February 1913, it has always found an enthusiastic audience, something which has been denied to many of Schoenberg's other works.

Schoenberg's next work, too, was based on a programme. The symphonic poem after Maeterlinck's drama *Pelleas und Melisande*, in one movement like the sextet *Verklaerte Nacht*, and lasting forty minutes (thus less than half the time of the *Gurrelieder*), in its language goes far beyond the 'fresco' style of the New German school. Schoenberg's nature, introverted and urging him towards the highest intensity of artistic creation, took him for a short period along the same path as Richard Strauss. The *Gurrelieder* are an expression of this influence; in *Pelleas* they have been conquered. But Debussy's purely expres-

[1] Composer and conductor, 1878-1934.

sive and as it were 'static' treatment of the atmosphere of a subject would also have appeared insufficient to him had he known the music of the Frenchman. For the analyst of style it is a happy coincidence that the two versions of the same subject were created contemporaneously and yet independently. Debussy creates a lyrical drama—an opera of moods of twilight and shadow, from whose diffuse world of sound a new impressionistic aesthetic was derived and became extremely fruitful. Schoenberg always thinks as an absolute musician, even where he illustrates and uses illustrative musical effects. He achieves here a polyphonic style and links his themes in a way which reminds one of Brahms or sometimes of Max Reger. The language of harmony goes far beyond that of the earlier works. The chromatic web of chords is developed with a masterly sureness to the limits of tonality, and unresolved suspensions and altered notes are made to serve contrapuntal purposes. The polyphony of themes is enlarged to become poly-chordal. By the use of chromatic contrary motion of augmented triads, six-part chords emerge which, deprived of any tonal function, open up the area of the whole-tone scale. For the first time chords built on fourths appear.

Difficult to define tonally, these are to play an important part in a number of Schoenberg's later works, and through them the system of harmony built up in thirds fixed by Jean Phillippe Rameau is shaken. How much Schoenberg's imagination also penetrates instrumental technique is shown by his introduction of the sinister trombone glissandi—an effect which was later much used in symphonic as well as jazz music. In no phase of his later development did Schoenberg come closer to a synthesis of illustrative tone-painting and symphonic polyphony in the spirit of the Viennese School.

With the score of *Pelleas* his first creative period ends. It is a period which as it were paraphrases the world of expression of the New German school, which uses the pictorial and the literary programme as a formal stimulus, and exhausts the associative possibilities of tone and sound with an extraordinary power of aesthetic feeling. The radicalism of 'thinking right through to the end' which remained a characteristic of Schoenberg's development in all phases is expressed here in a summation of pictorial and orchestral means which cannot be heightened further. Schoenberg ended this period with a sudden, abrupt change: what followed next was aimed at totally different ends. His way of living too was now changing. The Berlin episode was over. Vienna, his real home, received the twenty-nine-year-old composer: new people and new activities awaited him and brought him new impulses, but also difficulties.

FIRST CRISIS

V<small>IENNA</small> in the first decade of the twentieth century was the collecting point of avant-garde ideas in every sector of the arts. A young generation of revolutionary spirits entered the arena, eager to assert their demand for artistic truth in the face of a lazy satisfied public thirsting for nothing but conventional beauty. Here the architect Adolf Loos drafted the first plans for houses and offices whose lack of ornamentation upset the admirers of the baroque or Renaissance styles as much as the apostles of the Jugendstil (art nouveau). Here young Oskar Kokoschka was trying his hand; his portraits ruthlessly sacrificed the pleasing exterior of his subject, to arrive all the more expressively beneath the surface, and thus by ingeniously linking the feeling for composition and psychological intuition achieved a new form of painting. Here the brain of Karl Kraus, the polemical writer, was whetted; in his *Fackel* ('The Torch') he was to declare bitter war on everything untrue and unreal in literature, journalism, and politics. Here lived the young dream-lyricist, Hugo von Hofmannsthal, and the poetic impressionist and essayist, Peter Altenberg.[1] The Vienna 'Secession' (a picture gallery) had become accepted by society. Siegmund Freud developed his new psychology; Hermann Bahr rapidly took hold of every new intellectual phenomenon, looked at it, publicised it and made it famous.

Compared with this galaxy of modern ideas music appeared

---

[1] A Viennese poet (1859-1919) who was in the habit of sending 'scandalous' postcards to his friends or enemies. Berg set some of these postcard texts in his opus 4 for voice and orchestra.

conservative. Certainly the Wagnerians, driven on by the followers of Bruckner and Hugo Wolf, had sharply fought against the rigid academism of the traditionalists, and, on the other side, not all those belonging to the Brahms group were unconditionally opposed to new ideas. But the leading institutions, the musical academies, represented a spirit which tried if possible to outdo the conservatism of the Leipzig or Paris conservatoires. The extraordinarily powerful and intellectually well organised music criticism of Vienna was forced by Hanslick into a front of opposition against anything that was novel.

Originally even the Hofoper (Imperial Opera) was a fortress of this conservative spirit. But since 1897 Gustav Mahler had been first its conductor and then its director. And Mahler was anything but a classicist; his fiery spirit would not tolerate anything which was comfortably based on unchanging traditions. With his uncompromising spirit he took the side of the young men who were engaged in the fight against the spirit of petty bourgeois backwardness. These young men treated him with god-like devotion, for they were grateful to him for performances of operas and concerts in which the works were performed with incomparable intensity and fanatical precision. The Wagner performances that Schoenberg heard in his early years must have been unforgettable, and the picture of Gustav Mahler was inseparably linked with his impression of these operatic evenings.

When Schoenberg returned to Vienna in July of 1903, only two musicians were living there to whom he could feel close spiritually: Gustav Mahler and Alexander von Zemlinksy. With the latter, as in former years, he spent the summer in the country, where he continued the instrumentation of the *Gurrelieder*. The year also brought sketches for a choral work and a string quartet, both of which remained uncompleted.

Schenker

Schoenberg: the Berlin years.

Schoenberg's Master Class in Berlin, May 1926.
Left to right: Adolphe Weiss, Walter Goehr, Walter Gronostai,
Schmid, Winfried Zillig, Josef Rufer (in front) Schoenberg and
Zmigrod (Allan Gray)

Arnold Schoenberg and Winfried Zillig in Lugano (1931)

But Schoenberg's activity as a teacher now took a decisive turn. Courses in musical composition were arranged for him in the much-discussed Schwarzwald Schools. These were teaching institutions, guided by new educational and social ideas, which were set up at that time, and whose extraordinarily fruitful work Dr Eugenie Schwarzwald continued until shortly before Hitler's seizure of power in Vienna. They found an enthusiastic echo among the progressive spirits of the younger generation.

Alban Berg, Erwin Stein, Anton von Webern and Egon Wellesz became his pupils at this time; these four musicians carried the ideas of his teaching further, partly in the creative, partly in the practical and musicological fields. Alban Berg, the strongest artistic personality of the circle, had in a similar way to Schoenberg himself, sacrificed a bourgeois civil service career so as to dedicate himself entirely to music. An enthusiastic, passionate nature, he tended in his early works to a certain neo-romantic voluptuousness and sensuousness of sound which derived from Wagner and which still dominates the *Seven Early Songs* and the piano sonata. Under Schoenberg's influence his style developed into a maturity and mastery which made it possible for him to write *Wozzeck*—one of the most important operas of the century—the *Lyric Suite* for string quartet and the violin concerto. A greater contrast can hardly be imagined than that between Berg and the slightly older Webern; the former had a personality open to the world, moved by dramatic conflicts and tending towards sybaritism; the latter was a quiet introverted man of the type of a kindly young country priest. Webern later deduced the most radical inferences from the style of the middle period of Schoenberg; in their amazing brevity his chamber and orchestral works are true compressions of the *espressivo* style, aphorisms in sound in whose fleeting forms a microcosm of musical experience is compressed. Both Berg and Webern, who loved their master

c

with an unchanging faith, died untimely deaths—the former on 24 December 1935 as a result of blood-poisoning, the latter on 15 September 1945 by the bullet of a soldier of the occupation forces.

What the creative, educational, aesthetic and practical discussion with these uncommon spirits who had sought his instruction meant for Schoenberg, is shown by his *Treatise on Harmony* (*Harmonielehre*). This book, which was only written down some time between 1910 and 1911, is the fruit of his teaching experience, which reaches back to 1902, and which forced him towards a clearer formulation of theoretical problems. In his own words, Schoenberg had 'learnt it from his pupils'; and in his final chapters he underlines the community of creative experience which linked him with Berg and Webern, and also with musicians outside his own circle, such as Franz Schreker and Béla Bartók. Certain harmonic phenomena for which there was no 'explanation' within the framework of traditional teaching are ascribed by him to a feeling of necessity. In this sense of a creed, of a spiritual exhibition, this textbook is far more than a catechism for instructing pupils. It is a creative document of this crisis of the time, that between the turn of the century and the first world war, under whose sign every new art form found itself. For the spiritual development of the author it is remarkable that this final discussion of traditional theory was only expressed in thought when he had long since gone beyond it creatively.

For the music which was being composed by Schoenberg while the *Harmonielehre* was being written is the music of a further period of development. The works which correspond to the stage of the realisation of the textbook, and thus in fact embody the process of the crisis, were written several years earlier. In them there is contained the slow process of emancipation, painful detaching of the self from loved tradi-

tions, the casting away of shrouds and coverings, behind which
the face of the daemon becomes increasingly more visible.

The period from 1903 to 1908 was marked externally by
teaching activities, which took up more and more time in
Schoenberg's life. Usually composing was put off till the
summer months, which were spent in Moedling in 1904, the
following year in Gmunden on the Traunsee, in 1906 in
Tegernsee, in 1908 again in Gmunden. In 1906 Schoenberg's
first son, Georg, who now lives in Moedling near Vienna, was
born. The friendship with Mahler, sometimes clouded by deep
differences of opinion, underwent the stress of separation in
1907, when the older man left Vienna for New York. During
that year Schoenberg began to draw and to paint. Pushed on
by the same daemonic compulsion as that governing his music,
some extremely odd pictures resulted, visions of a fantasy
world resembling that of Alfred Kubin[1]: masks; a portrait of a
woman; several self-portraits—one of them of his back. Later
on, at an exhibition in Vienna, the paintings were admired by
many famous people. Wassily Kandinsky made them the
subject of a profoundly analytical essay about Schoenberg's
personality.

Yet Schoenberg's music still lacked a wide reputation.
Certainly Arnold Rosé had played the sextet for the first time
in the Vienna Tonkuenstlerverein in 1903: but the need of
systematically furthering new music was proved over and over
again by the lack of understanding by the critics and many
listeners. So, as early as 1904, the 'Union of Creative Musicians'
was founded, grouping together, under Mahler's honorary
presidency, Rudolf St Hoffmann, Gerhard von Keussler, Oskar
C. Posa, Schoenberg, Bruno Walter, Karl Weigl, Joseph

---

[1] A painter who belonged to the 'Blaue Reiter' group in Munich, together
with Klee and Kandinsky; their first exhibition, in 1911, also contained
some pictures by Schoenberg.

Venantius von Woess and Alexander Zemlinsky. Under their auspices Schoenberg conducted the first performance of *Pelleas und Melisande* in January 1905. It met with the same lack of understanding as other first performances of his works. The Union, under whose auspices first performances also took place of works by Siegmund von Hausegger (*Dionysische Phantasie*), Mahler (*Kindertoten* and *Wunderhornlieder*), Richard Strauss (*Sinfonia Domestica*) and Zemlinsky (*Seejungfrau*), was dissolved during the same year.

In his creative work Schoenberg remained untouched by this lack of success. During the summers of 1904 and 1905 he worked on the mighty structure of his first string quartet opus 7. It was Schoenberg's first attempt in the realm of absolute music; formally its four movements (which however have no breaks between them) are a faithful copy of classical forms, with a special leaning towards Beethoven. Melodically and harmonically it is close to the style of the sextet, though in its polyphony it is nearer that of *Pelleas*. Forty years later (in the book *Style and Idea*) Schoenberg pointed to the spontaneity with which he had improvised the most complicated counterpoints and the most distant thematic-motivic relations. There is no doubt that opus 7 is full of intoxicating inspiration, as is shown, for example, by the big E major theme of the adagio, which can be ranked with many great examples of romantic music. With this work he has almost reached the limits of romantic expression. And this has been done strictly by the means of chamber music, forgoing the mass effects of the orchestral apparatus, whose polychromaticism was the stylistic nucleus of a contemporary work such as Richard Strauss's *Salome*. Schoenberg here faces the law of limitation (whose use by Goethe he later once polemically attacked); in opus 7 he translates the compositional experiences of the mammoth sound organism into classical four-part writing which, never-

theless, appears filled out by chords, through a subtle use of
string technique.

The next work was a volume of Lieder—as so often in
Schoenberg's early period, as a break after work on large
forms. But it is not the collection of six orchestral songs, which
is known as opus 8, but the eight Lieder opus 6. Again he uses
verses from the new German poets, Dehmel, Julius Hart, John
Henry Mackay; but Nietzsche's *Wanderer* and a ghazel by
Goffried Keller[1] were also included. Schoenberg's skill in
thematic work and variation can best be studied in the ghazel:

Here he develops from a chromatic three-note motif a
movement which, using imitation, deviation, augmentation
and diminution, runs in parallel with the text, sometimes as a
canto fermo, sometimes as an accompanying figure, and this
proves the liveliness of the Brahmsian tradition as well as the
creative imagination of the man who deduced the most fateful
consequences from it. In point of time the composition of these
songs coincides more or less with the sketching of a quintet
which was to remain unfinished, as were also the drafts of an
opera based on Gerhart Hauptmann's[2] fairy tale *Und Pippa
Tanzt*.

The summer of 1906, spent on the Tegernsee, produced
work whose stylistic influence on the whole of modern music
was not to be foreseen—the chamber symphony for fifteen
solo instruments, opus 9, in E major. Reacting against the
contemporary super-orchestras (six years before Richard

---

[1] Swiss poet, 1819-1890.
[2] 1862-1945.

Strauss tried something similar in *Ariadne auf Naxos*) this score
is not merely something quite unexpected on the surface; the
strongly individual procedure shown in the scoring for solo
instruments only is characteristic of the whole of Schoenberg's
spiritual world and his surroundings. In addition opus 9 lays
down new harmonic and melodic forms which point beyond
the crisis itself towards future procedures. The six-part chord,
based on fourths

whose notes, transposed a fifth higher, at once appear as a
theme, are the forerunner of the serial method, which much
later acquired a new decisive function in twelve-note music. It
combines half of the circle of fifths into one chord and one
theme; its notes as such can still be heard 'diatonically', but as
a result of their arrangement in fourths they deny the principle
of diatonic writing and also that of tonality to a considerable
extent. The chord is still treated tonally; in a quick modulation
Schoenberg resolves it evasively into F major, the A flat in
the alto part acting as a leading note to A. Such chromatic
'side-slips' with the feeling of a leading note, in which every
note in a chord can be regarded as an anticipation of its neighbouring notes above or below, are a stylistic mark of the first
importance in the music of Schoenberg's middle period.

In the *Georgelieder* above all they occupy an important place.
Their function is only apparently a tonal one; in reality they
break up key-feeling more and more, since by this means
(which in older music was achieved only through the Neapoli-
tan sixth) every desired resolution of discords is possible
without however establishing a predominant tonality. To the

fourth chords should be added the harmonic and melodic use of the whole-tone scale.

Within this extraordinarily relaxed tonality, in a harmony of surprising freedom and constant alteration, Schoenberg keeps to the tonal laws of sonata structure; there are tonic-and-dominant relations, subsidiary themes, reprises, developments, and the five sections which flow into one another without a break keep to the movements of a classical sonata, and also in their totality form an expanded sonata movement.

The fourth-chord appears at once, split up into a rising theme which introduces the main movement, and followed by an equally passionate mounting theme in whole tones, modulating from E through many degrees of the scale. A second idea in F minor follows as a contrast; the ideas are developed with complex motivic treatment and follow the principle of constant variation which even then governed Schoenberg's technique of composition.

A short transition prepares for the 'second subject' ('Viel langsamer als das erste Zeitmass'), which begins at figure 21 in the score—very song-like, an A major melody of romantic lyricism, in contrary motion to a beautifully moving bass. This theme, although invented as a contrast to the main section, is related to it motivically, through the dotted rhythm of a rising three-note figure. The final section of this first, broad exposition movement repeats the main theme more briefly and in a varied form, and a ('noch ruhiger') chordal transition works up from triads to very characteristic ninth- and eleventh-chords and leaps into the Scherzo with a fortissimo sequence of thirds.

This second section, very fast, 3/4 in basic metre (in spite of frequent changes of time) and in C minor, with two ostinato percussive motifs which answer each other polyrhythmically, is followed by a still faster trio, after which comes the development of the scherzo motifs. With a constant accelerando the scherzo ends with its reprise, which at number 60 ('Viel langsamer, aber doch fliessend') is followed by the third section of the work.

This is the real development section; in three extensive parts it subjects the thematic material heard so far in the exposition and scherzo to numberless processes of variation.

In regrouping of motifs, in harmonic and rhythmic changes, in mirror forms of intervals and contrapuntal interweavings, Schoenberg here carries the development of the late Beethoven to its boldest consequences. The fourth-theme, also, with its rising and falling sequence of intervals, both melodically and harmonically, gains an increasing importance at the end of the development section. It comes at the beginning of the fourth main section, after figure 77 ('Viel langsamer'), where it dominates ten fantasia-like introductory bars, which resemble the beginning of the whole work and lead to the real adagio section ('Fliessender').

The theme of the slow section begins on an up-beat in 4/4 and is sequential: it is almost impossible to define tonally, even though G forms a certain centre of gravity in the harmonic tissue. In contrast to it (figure 86, 'etwas bewegter') a second idea appears in B major, altered by whole-tone scales. The motivic material of both ideas is developed and quickly leads to the fifth section. With it, at number 90 ('Schwungvoll'), the finale is reached. This begins with a reprise of the theme from the first transitional passage just before the 'second subject' in the exposition. The themes of the first section are once again subjected to a development in which Schoenberg's ability to determine tonalities by periphrasis rather than by cadences achieves its acme. The 'second subject' dominates the last part of the final section; after a reprise of the inverted (descending) fourth-theme the main idea is quoted once more, and in a very fast, stretto-like motion the coda moves in a very complex cadence towards the final chord of E major.

According to Schoenberg's own testimony the work was much revised in some sections; others were written down spontaneously.

(Simultaneously with this chamber symphony he also began a second one in E flat minor, which remained half completed at the time. Its sketches went with Schoenberg to the United States, where in 1940—thirty-four years later—he finished it.) Together with a reduction of the orchestra to one each of flute (also playing piccolo), oboe, English horn, D (also E flat) clarinet, A (also B flat) clarinet, bass-clarinet, bassoon, contra-bassoon, two horns, two violins, viola, cello and bass, this work shows a reduction in weight and a turning away from heavy rhetoric. The first chamber symphony is only half as long as the early chamber music works and orchestral and choral pieces. Its character is lively, light and energetic. Even the cantabile subsidiary theme in A major, despite all its intensity of melodic tension, no longer has anything of the heated over-dramatisation of the earlier works. Here, in the midst of an incredible intellectual process of relaxation of key, there can be felt a striving for clear contours, a lucidity of expression and a mastering of the *espressivo* style.

The first performance of the chamber symphony in 1907 (in the same year as that of the quartet opus 7) was given by the Rosé quartet and the wind ensemble of the Hofoper in Vienna, and caused a huge scandal. In the course of this year, which also saw Mahler's departure from Vienna, several works of less importance were written—the mixed *a cappella* chorus *Friede auf Erden*, one of the Ballads opus 12, and one of the Lieder opus 14. But the crisis became manifest in the two decisive works of the transitional period which were composed in part simultaneously and were completed shortly one after the other. They are the F sharp minor string quartet opus 10 and the Stefan George Lieder opus 15. Closely linked with them stylistically are the two Lieder opus 14, which also belong to the years 1907 and 1908. (The opus numbers in Schoenberg's case do not correspond to the dates of composition, as in part they were assigned according to the order of publication; for example, opus 11 was written between opus 15 and 16.)

The quartet in F sharp minor contains a considerable number of novelties: in the last two movements a soprano voice is added to the four strings. In spite of its four movements the traditional form is discarded, particularly in the two movements with voice; harmony glides in long stretches beyond the frontiers of traditional tonality into a new foreign world of sound relations for which no law had hitherto been found. Schoenberg was still basing himself on chord forms which belong to the world of major and minor keys; the quartet opens and ends tonally, and frequently shows forms of harmony similar to cadences. But, in between, sounds and groups of sounds exist which in fact appear to stem 'from other planets' like the air of which the text by Stefan George[1] (*Entrueckung*) for the finale of the quartet tells us.

The chords without 'function' (in the sense of Hugo Riemann), without 'correct' resolution or development, are not an exclusive invention of Schoenberg's. They appear simultaneously or earlier in Debussy and Janáček, in Skriabin and Bartók. But Debussy arrives at them in a purely 'sound-experimental' way, while in Schoenberg's case they are arrived at and used creatively as the final result of a long chain of chromatic alteration, shortening of harmonic processes and elliptical modulation. Together with this increasing use of

[1] 1868-1934. A Rhineland poet who lived in Paris, Berlin and Munich; chief of a group of German poets who were much influenced by Baudelaire and Mallarmé.

untried sounds and sound forms, which are still fresh in their adventurous attraction, goes a change in the sphere of expression. The *espressivo* style, as inherited by Gustav Mahler from the late romantic world of Wagner and passed on to Schoenberg, had already gone beyond the zenith of its possibilities in the *Gurrelieder*. A heightening of emotional experience was imaginable only as an introversion, a turning inwards. The rhetorical cries and outbursts of music-drama give way to a less vital, a more 'plant-like' sensibility. It is no accident that in this phase of his development Schoenberg leans repeatedly on the measured, highly formalised, esoteric lyricism of Stefan George, who considers all noisy gestures as profane and hateful. His music, though, is far removed from such sublimity; it shows bizarreness and capriciousness of character, of which the quotation of 'O du lieber Augustin' in the second movement of the quartet in F sharp minor is typical.

The make-up of this work is determined far more by the sound and by the individual chord than the D minor quartet or the chamber symphony are. In place of the hitherto dominant counterpoint there can be found here an extraordinary transparency of texture, a chamber music approach which reminds one of Haydn and Mozart, and which achieves its climax in the final movement within a world of great tonal freedom.

In form the third movement, the 'Litanei', shows certain links with the traditional sonata plan. It consists of free variations, which may be regarded as a development section in the classical Beethovenian sense. The theme

has been derived from the F sharp minor theme of the first movement with slight rhythmical variation.

The last movement, the above-mentioned *Entrueckung*, is of great importance as the seed of several later turns in Schoenberg's development. It is a free fantasy linked closely to the poem, with outlines which are sharpened towards the end. René Leibowitz has pointed out that the beginning of this movement

is free from all tonal ties and anticipates the serial technique of Schoenberg's twelve-note music. In fact all twelve notes constantly appear here, closely compressed and with a minimum of repetition. Doubtless this step was entirely guided by intuition, just as all of Schoenberg's discoveries and innovations are the product of a feeling, a compulsion, and an inner vision, which were recognised later and catalogued by orderly intelligence. Schoenberg has himself repeatedly pointed to this compulsion ('Art comes from necessity'—'Kunst kommt von Müssen'), when opponents accused him of cerebral construction, though he also constantly guarded against underestimating the intellect. In December 1908, shortly after its completion, the first performance of the F sharp minor quartet by the Rosé Quartet and Marie Gutheil-Schoder, the famous singer of the Vienna Hofoper, took place in the Boesendorfersaal in front of an audience that was uncomprehending, noisy and laughed derisively.

Simultaneously with the second quartet were written the 'Fifteen Poems from *Das Buch der haengenden Gaerten* by Stefan George'. This, opus 15, is spiritually a continuation of the great romantic Lieder cycles of Beethoven, Schubert and Schumann. For Schoenberg it was a decisive work. Here (in his own words) he was 'for the first time successful in coming near an ideal of expression and form which I had had in mind ("mir Vorschwebt") for years. But up to that point I had lacked the strength and certainty to realise it. Now that I have finally embarked upon this path I am conscious that I have broken all barriers of a past aesthetic.' The composer wrote these words in the programme of the first performance. What had appeared in the chamber symphony and in the F sharp minor quartet only as an occasional divergence, even if used in long passages, is here completely carried through and used as a starting point: it is the liquidation of tonality. In these fifteen pieces no functional relationship of chords exists any longer; the triad too is now only used as an equal, no longer as a dominating harmony. Nevertheless the sound-effect of this music is still full of apparently tonal moments, and in some chord-sequences there are still memories of a tonal cadence. The fifth of the Lieder, *Saget mir, auf welchem Pfad heute sie vorueberschreite*, ends with a kind of G major cadence,

which is very strongly stressed by the bass fifth D-G, and which cannot be weakened by the chromatic movements in the upper parts (something similar occurs in the final bars of the tenth

Lied). Yet no tonal interpretation of the whole of the Lied is possible; G major is introduced here only as a means of expression, and its functional power is much smaller than that of the predominantly chromatic use of notes with avoidance of cadences. The system of the 'leading-note relation' in all notes, the advance with the use of semi-tonal movement in several parts, in parallel or contrary motion, is of decisive importance in the *Georgelieder*. It replaces to a large extent the functional relationship of the chords. In an analysis of the harmonic progressions one frequently gets the impression of a strange force of suction which is inherent in these sounds and which forces them into certain motions. It is something like a physical phenomenon, a kind of 'osmosis' of sound, in which it does not matter whether the progression leads to a triad or an unanalysable dissonance. A typical example of this 'chord-osmosis' is the resolution of a six-part fourth-chord into an E major 6/3 chord in the sixth Lied, at the tempo mark 'Langsamer'.

In form the Lieder are of great freedom; in some the outlines of two- and three-part Lied forms are still recognisable, in others one finds canonic and imitative passages. But the majority are pure imaginative forms, in which the utterly logical effect and unforced appearance of the structure seem almost a puzzling phenomenon. Some of these Lieder are linked by certain thematic and motivic relationships, and the basic style of the work gives them a stylistic completeness, which mingles in a fascinating manner with that of Stefan George's verses. Like a tragic summing-up of all the melodic, harmonic and rhythmic tension which belongs to them, the fifteenth and last of the Lieder is built up with a greatness and power of melody to which no well-disposed listener can be indifferent.

But Schoenberg spoke not only of an ideal of form, but also of an ideal of expression. Music and text undergo a mystic marriage. As poems the *Georgelieder* deal with tragic events. Like the programme of *Verklaerte Nacht*, like the most intimate parts of the *Gurrelieder*, they are an intimate occasion of a subtle, esoteric kind. In George's poems the park landscape in which they are set reveals a bewitching, sultry, exotic magic. Two people are here, a man, respectful, shy and loving with a growing longing, and a woman of priestess-like aristocratic exaltation, who finally leaves this bewitched unfortunate. The way in which Schoenberg mirrors the changing soul- and nature-moods of these poems in sounds far removed from all naturalistic sound-painting, merely by the unison of word and music, is a new experience from bar to bar.

In the cycle song and piano have equal rights. Both are treated in a totally novel manner. The dynamics and phrasing demand a new sensibility going far beyond traditional conceptions. The voice is exposed to a number of problems; it is taken from the lower register of an alto straight to the high notes of a soprano, and has to master difficulties of intonation where the piano more often acts as an obstacle than a help.

For Schoenberg the *Georgelieder* were decisive; after them he composed only a few Lieder (four orchestral Lieder opus 22 and three Lieder for low voice opus 48). In this cycle music enters on a new era of free expression. It affects us with the same strength as other great works of art of the same period: Richard Strauss's *Elektra*, Rainer Maria Rilke's *Stundenbuch*, Claude Debussy's *Préludes*, Pablo Picasso's and Georges Braque's early cubist painting, Oskar Kokoschka's psychological portraits and the paintings of the Dresden 'Bruecke' circle.

Yet this music still echoes the spirit of *Tristan*. But the rhetoric has turned inwards; the soprano part only moves in the manner of a lightning eruption, never in that of a broad dramatic climax, and its position and register are ruled by extremes. The fever chart of this music changes constantly from dreamlike twilight to cries of quickly silenced passion. The crisis is no longer latent. An irrevocable step has been taken; with the *Georgelieder* the whole of modern music has entered upon a new phase of development.

Meeting in a Berlin bar.
Left to right: Adolf Loos, Arnold Schoenberg, Frau Gertrud
Schoenberg and Oskar Kokoschka

Self Portrait

THE STYLE OF FREEDOM

THE 'BREAKING OF ALL BARRIERS OF A PAST AESTHETIC' was a process of incredible difficulty for a man such as Schoenberg with a deep feeling of responsibility for his craft. In his *Harmonielehre* he describes how he often hesitated before writing down a chord for which he could not account. Yet at the same time he was conscious of the irrevocability of this breakthrough. Today we know that this process was not only subjectively justified by Schoenberg's genius, but that it was a historical necessity, that since the introducton of the tempered system about 1700 the development of harmony was resolutely striving towards the results which Schoenberg had the courage to present to the world.

In the reactionary musical circles of Vienna these results could evoke nothing but horror. People regarded their inventor as a wild nihilist, contemptuous of all laws, a 'coffee-house Bohemian', who out of wantonness and disgust with the conventional wrote something just for the sake of being different. Certainly in the discovery of new harmonic, melodic and formal phenomena the moment of disgust and irritation played a part too: that has been the case at all times with all progressive cultures. Ferruccio Busoni, the pianist of genius and champion of 'music of the future', wrote his *Sketch for a new aesthetic of music* in 1906, thus at about the time of Schoenberg's works of crisis. Here this important sentence can be found: 'The task of the creator consists in establishing laws and not in following laws'. But Busoni, with his romantically motivated spirit, was far more prone to Utopia, to speculation,

D   49

and to a desire for new things out of sheer boredom than the basically conservative Schoenberg. The spoilt international virtuoso lived in a world of success which did not satisfy him and from which he took refuge in an atmosphere of highly cerebral composition. Schoenberg's external world was strictly limited, it was modest; he had learned early to do without success, and to be satisfied with that praise which all creative work finds in itself. His everyday life was strictly regulated. Though Schoenberg never composed at fixed times of day (as did his opposite pole Igor Stravinsky), he was constantly occupied with productive work. The task he had set himself was more important than life; the architect Adolf Loos, who was linked in a long and close friendship with Schoenberg, experienced this once in a drastic manner when Schoenberg interrupted a social occasion with the remark that he had to get to his desk. Schoenberg's disciplined existence found no time for Bohemian habits, and even the most apparently burdensome conversation with pupils and friends always served to help solve a spiritual, aesthetic or creative problem. So that in the picture of his personality every trace of frivolity is missing. One could almost say that this was a lack—a very German defect in Schoenberg, that he was incapable of making light of anything. Even his most sarcastic remarks and polemical battles are weighed down by serious thought.

The throwing off of one chain of tradition after another is of special importance with a man of this kind. Those years in which Schoenberg succeeded in breaking through the barriers of an existing aesthetic were brimful of every kind of activity. They were the years of the most thorough discussion and explanation of pedagogic questions, during which Berg and Webern received a system of instruction as strict as it was many-sided (Berg at this time wrote the *Sieben fruehe Lieder* and the piano sonata opus 1, Webern the orchestral passacaglia);

besides numerous compositions and writings the majority of Schoenberg's paintings were done at this time and in addition there were his activities as a conductor.

The piano pieces opus 11, in spite of their low opus number, were composed in 1908, at the same time as the *Georgelieder*, and occupy an important place in the creative work of that year. In the same way as Schoenberg had detached himself from the chains of programme music with the first string quartet opus 7, and had turned towards the forms of absolute music, so here he relinquished the support of poetry set to music, which in the preceding work had eased the leap into a completely new world of sound. The three piano pieces, and especially the last one, proceed on the path towards a completely free style of themelessness—a direction which some of the *Georgelieder* had already indicated. To forgo thematic and motivic repetitions, which only occur sporadically as immediate repetitions of short note-sequences, brings the danger of chaos and lack of technical control. This is caused by the desire not to repeat anything once stated, and to subjugate the form of music solely to a law of feeling. A highly tense melodic line, linked to a world of sound which touches hidden depths of the psyche, here forms an expression of great intimacy, an expressive language of unusual concentration. This truly new music contains something aphoristic, something compressed into its essence, for which no example or parallel exists in the audacity of its consequences, but which continues in spirit the line of some of Bach's fantasias (such as the opening of the Chromatic Fantasia). In the piano writing the influence of Brahms, with his widely spread out broken chords, is to be found. The harmony is free from all tonal ties; the melody, as often with Schoenberg, is based on 'notes foreign to the harmony', big intervals and widely spaced undulatory movements. The much-discussed piano harmonics here used by Schoenberg, achieved by depressing four notes silently, whose strings are only made to vibrate by depressing the same notes in a lower octave, go further than a similar sound-experiment of Schumann's.

An important formal characteristic of the piano pieces is their brevity and their utter economy of means. This is also important in the style of the next work, the five orchestral pieces opus 16, composed at the beginning of 1909; Schoenberg completed the score that summer in Steinakirchen near Amstetten in lower Austria. In one of the five pieces— originally they had been meant to bear such titles as *Vorgefuehle* (Presentiments) or *Das obligate Rezitativ* (The obbligato recitative)—the dimension of time in the musical sense is almost done away with. There is no longer any material development worth mentioning; instead the piece consists of a five-part chord whose effect is changed only by constantly varying instrumentation.

Schoenberg here translates into reality the thoughts which he had formulated in the last sentences of the *Harmonielehre*, that music in future would use tone-colour to create melody. In a conversation with Gustav Mahler he discussed the idea of forming a melody by presenting a note in changing tone-colours. The effect of this third orchestral piece is not of course 'melodic'; it exercises a charm of a new and special kind, a charm of a sound-impression, which also occurs occasionally in Debussy in a more moderate form. Like the piano pieces opus 11, this score is governed by complete formal freedom. The themes are still developed in some instances, but with the greatest brevity and without relation to traditional forms. As opposed to the piano pieces, the greater breadth of the polyphonic texture, the chamber-music-like clarity of counterpoint and the singing character of the melodic material are remarkable, particularly in the second and fifth pieces. Schoenberg here introduces signs for the main and subsidiary parts so as to arrange the parts in order of importance; these have since given all his scores great clarity. The completely new kind of instrumentation, which particularly likes to combine contrasting solo instruments, and if possible in unusual registers, into chords and counterpoints, makes this aid for the players and conductor necessary. A particularly striking effect, which was still unknown in 1909, is the *fff* tremolo of muted trombones and bass-tuba in the first piece. These five orchestral pieces were not performed till 1912, and then not in Schoenberg's own country, but in London at a Promenade Concert conducted by Sir Henry Wood in the Queen's Hall.

In the summer Schoenberg composed feverishly. In the seventeen days between August 27 and September 12 his first stage work was written—the monodrama *Erwartung*, based on a text of Marie Pappenheim. The work, which lasts for about half an hour, is written for female voice and large orchestra (quadruple to quintuple woodwind, triple to quadruple brass, harp, celesta, a good deal of percussion and strings). The text is in the form of a monologue; it describes the feelings of a woman who seeks her lover at night in the wood and finally finds him dead. Through the visions of her overheated imagination, which is full of presentiments, the impressions of nature at night time, and the changes between fear, hope and cruel knowledge, the feeling of the text has been raised to a plane of hectic exaggeration, whose language anticipates forms of expressionistic poetry which only became common much later. In both text and music it is an attempt to describe a microcosm of feeling and mood which hundreds of changing moods of passion rush through at great speed—perhaps something like the consciousness of a dying man who sees the whole of his life rolling past him like a fast-moving film.

Musically this happens in the harmonic field, which shows a penchant for the unknown and the incredible, and carefully avoids any suggestion of normal aesthetic 'to please'. The chords which occur most frequently are clusters of seconds, altered fourth-chords and complexes of six to eleven different notes. The rhythm has achieved a degree of flowing freedom which overrides all limitations of the bar-line, and which constantly combines triplets and sextuplets with numerous subdivisions and punctuations. The melody is paramount above all the other elements—it is a vocal melody of a highly expressive but quite revolutionary kind. It is totally independent of the harmony, following its own laws and polyphonic tensions —a powerful pulsating organism of reverberating waves, whose fever chart fluctuates constantly between extremes. It has been pointed out that the whole of *Erwartung* can be compared in form to a pre-Wagnerian opera finale or to a 'scene and aria'.

In fact the piece is free from any kind of symphonic working out, and at first glance appears amorphous. Nevertheless, even if it is devoid of any Wagnerian Leitmotif symbolism, certain chord and melodic phenomena exist which constantly recur in the score, and which as 'idées fixes' influence the completely free structure of the opera. The ascending phrase D–F–C-sharp must be regarded as the cornerstone in this sense, repeatedly used in rhythmic variants and transpositions. Pedal points and prolonged ostinato repetitions of note-sequences appear frequently. As a negative stylistic point, the avoidance of octave doublings is dominant in *Erwartung*; in their place there appears as favoured intervals major sevenths, minor ninths and augmented fourths. The part is written for a youthful dramatic soprano, and demands a degree of passionate expression and musicianship from the singer which is rarely found on the stage in Germany. It continues along the spiritual and musical line which began with Isolde and Kundry, and which had been widened with Salome and Elektra to a degree that apparently did not permit of further development. Nevertheless it would be wrong to catalogue the monodrama as a work of 'succession', as Paul Bekker[1] does in an essay that is otherwise deeply penetrating. In spirit, like its partner *Die Glueckliche Hand*, it belongs to a type of aphoristic, compressed music drama, imaginable only to an expert with knowledge of the most up-to-date modern psychological analysis, or a pioneer in the realm of dreams and the subconscious. In an extreme compression of time a spiritual realism of the most frightening kind is employed here, which points to the surrealist drama of the future rather than to the mystical music drama of the past.

Immediately following the composition of *Erwartung* Schoenberg wrote the libretto for his second work for the stage—*Die Glueckliche Hand*. It appeals to the same hidden layers of the subconscious without aiming at the spiritual tension of the monodrama. In the logical sense the text is without subject, without reality. It uses symbols, the play of colours (which are exactly fitted to the music), catlike mythical creatures, and a chorus which comments on the events in the manner of a Greek tragedy, and speaks directly to the main dramatic personage, 'the Man'. Here, too, the focal point is erotic tension: 'the Woman', who is passionately loved by 'the Man', turns to a third person, 'the Gentleman', and for 'the Man' (the only sung solo part in the work) there remains only pain and despair. Among the many novelties in the score a choral section is particularly striking, in which the voices

[1] Berlin critic and musicologist, 1882–1937.

speak in rhythmic polyphony only, as Schoenberg had already done with a solo voice in the *Gurrelieder*; this was soon to achieve a symptomatic importance in his creative work. The score of *Glueckliche Hand* was begun in 1910, but was not completed till three years later. In musical language it is closely related to *Erwartung*, far more closely than to the works which were written between 1910 and 1913.

With these two works for the stage, which were registered as opus 17 and 18, Schoenberg enormously advanced the development of opera. Their creation coincides with the years in which Richard Strauss turned away from the highly dramatic naturalistic expression of *Elektra* to the more restrained and elegant archaism of *Rosenkavalier*. Measured by the yardstick of their surroundings, they are the results of experiment and are attempts to achieve a new musical and dramatic style by totally novel means beyond realism. The stimulus which they gave to the compositions of the musicians of central Europe after the first world war cannot be over-estimated. Without this stimulus neither the early operas of Kurt Weill, nor those of Ernst Krenek (who in *Orpheus and Eurydike* clearly follows Schoenberg), nor the three one-act operas of Paul Hindemith, nor Alban Berg's *Wozzeck* would be conceivable.

An important event marked the beginning of 1910 for Schoenberg. The Union for Art and Culture in Vienna organised a concert in which the first part of the *Gurrelieder* (though only with piano accompaniment), the piano pieces opus 11 and the Stefan George Lieder were given in public for the first time. Martha Winternitz-Dorda, the mezzo-soprano (accompanied by Etta Werndorf), sang the *Georgelieder*. Among those taking part in the excerpt from the *Gurrelieder* were Anton von Webern and Rudolf Weirich as pianists; the tenor part was sung by Schoenberg's cousin, Hans Nachod.

The concert took place in the evening of 14 January in the Ehrbachsaal.

In 1910 Schoenberg achieved a somewhat questionable form of official recognition. The most devoted and the strictest teacher of his generation, he was 'permitted' to hold courses in composition at the Vienna Music Academy as lecturer extraordinary. In the course of this year he moved to more rural surroundings, to Ober St Veit near Vienna. A forthcoming exhibition of his paintings in the Heller Gallery stimulated him to take up painting again; in addition he worked on the score of *Gurrelieder*, and he began the writing down of the *Harmonielehre* and the composition of the *Glückliche Hand*. In the meantime in Berlin, Oskar Fried[1], one of the most active champions of modern music, had begun to notice Schoenberg. In October he performed *Pelleas und Melisande* in the presence of the composer in Berlin. This city, in which Busoni had also attracted a circle of progressive musicians around himself, once more exerted its somewhat cool charm on Schoenberg, and so perhaps sowed the seeds of the plan which he carried out the following summer—to leave Vienna and move his home once more to the German capital. In the autumn his last meeting with Gustav Mahler took place; he died on 18 May 1911. His death moved Schoenberg more than any other event of that year. In Mahler he lost not only the friendly champion of his early experiments, but a congenial companion, to whom even in moments of disagreement he was more closely linked than to the majority of his older contemporaries. The appreciation which he published in *Der Merker* expressed his grief as clearly as the last of the six little piano pieces opus 19, which was written under the immediate impression of the news of Mahler's death.

This opus 19 belongs to the key works in Schoenberg's

---

[1] Conductor and composer, 1871-1949.

development. If in the *Georgelieder* he had been successful in breaking through to new ideals of form and expression, the present phase of his life was spiritually expressed in the small piano pieces. The *espressivo* style is carried here to the limits of the immaterial. Each note is endowed with the weight of an experience. The most noticeable characteristic of these six pieces is their brevity: the longest, Number 1, consists of eighteen bars, the shortest, Numbers 2 and 3, only nine. Each one of these aphoristically brief structures incorporates a firmly outlined musical character, which is indicated by definite tempo markings (*Leicht, zart—Langsam—Sehr langsame Viertel —Rasch, aber leicht—Etwas rasch—Sehr langsam*) (Slow and tender—Slow—Very slow crotchets—Quick, but light—Fairly quick—Very slow). All tonal coherence has disappeared. The harmony goes up to six-part chords (the final chords of the second, fifth and sixth pieces). In general two- or three-part writing predominates. But there are also passages of solo melody accompanied by chords—as in the whole of the fourth piece. In the second piece a melody circles round an ostinato repeated third G-B; the third begins with a theme in the bass, broadly laid out and played *pp* throughout in octaves—a remarkable circumstance, since the writing in these works of Schoenberg's middle years generally avoids such doublings. Repetitions of themes and motifs are also almost completely excluded here, except perhaps in the fourth piece, where shortly before the end a variation in diminution of the opening theme appears. The last of the pieces achieves the furthest degree of dematerialisation of the musical language. It is nothing more than a tender short paraphrase on two chords which combine to make a six-part chord.

Five very small attempts at melodic formations take place; four of them consist of only two notes; another, five notes long, encompasses with true Schoenbergian intensity the space from high D down to the C sharp below middle C. The detailed markings prescribe dynamics from *p* to *pppp*.

The style of this work has found its strongest (or rather its most tender) echo in the music of Anton von Webern, which cannot be surpassed in immateriality, in brevity, and in the avoidance of anything that is loud and shallow musically.

In the spring of the year 1911 the score of the *Gurrelieder* was completed (eleven years after their composition was begun); in the summer work on the *Harmonielehre* was finished, and also several works of a musical-historical nature were completed. Schoenberg was then working on five scores of Viennese composers of the eighteenth century for the *Denkmaeler der Tonkust in Austria* ('Monuments of Music in Austria') edited by Guido Adler; a symphony, a cello concerto and two harpsichord concertos by Georg Matthias Monn[1] and a divertimento by Johann Christian Mann,[2] for which he realised the figured bass as a harpsichord part in a very artistic and thematic manner. Much later a concerto grosso by Handel was added to this group of works—Schoenberg arranged it for string quartet and orchestra in 1933—and he also made orchestral transcriptions of works by J. S. Bach (two chorale preludes, 1921; Prelude and Fugue in E flat major for organ, 1928) and Brahms (G minor piano quartet, opus 25).

[1] Composer from Lower Austria (1717-1750).
[2] Viennese composer (1726-1782).

'PIERROT LUNAIRE'

By THE SUMMER OF 1911 Schoenberg had moved to Berlin-Zehlendorf. He began a series of lectures in the autumn at the Stern Conservatoire, where, on the recommendation of Richard Strauss, he had already worked as a teacher nine years earlier. Among smaller compositions in 1911 the Lied *Herzgewaechse*, on a poem from Maurice Maeterlinck's *Serres chaudes*, was set for high coloratura soprano (to F in alt), celesta, harmonium and harp. In style it forms the link between the Small Piano Pieces and the next work—*Pierrot Lunaire*, which quickly became famous.

Schoenberg had met the actress Albertine Zehme in Berlin. She requested him to write a large-scale work for speaking voice. In March of 1912 he started on the composition of twenty-one 'melodramas' on poems of Albert Giraud, which had been translated into German by Otto Erich Hartleben.[1] The score was completed on 9 September, four days before his thirty-eighth birthday. During that summer Schoenberg started rehearsals for the first performance.

On 9 October the small Choralionsaal in Berlin's Bellevuestrasse, which was destroyed in 1945, was the scene of a dress rehearsal before an invited audience, including the Berlin Press. A week later the first public performance took place, Dark screens stood on the stage, and between them was Albertine Zehme in the costume of Colombine. Behind the scenes a handful of musicians conducted by Schoenberg played. As could be seen from the programme, they were Eduard

[1] German novelist and playwright of the late nineteenth century.

Steuermann (piano), Jakob Maliniak (violin), Hans Kindler (cello), H. W. de Fries (flute) and Karl Essberger (clarinet), all selected Berlin chamber musicians, among them members of the Royal Band and the Philharmonic Orchestra.

Max Marschalk wrote about the evening in the *Vossischer Zeitung*; he was then a disciple of Schoenberg and his first publisher. From his detailed discussion it can be learned that the performance—to the astonishment of the critics—resulted in an ovation for Schoenberg. The greater part of the audience remained in the hall after the end of the performance and forced a repeat. And that, in spite of the fact that Marschalk regarded the performance as 'incomplete to a considerable degree'. According to this critic's view this was not the fault of the excellent performance of the musicians, but that of the speaker, whom he considered as lacking in technique and interpretation, so that it was impossible to tell whether her performance represented unsuccessful speech or singing. Almost throughout the effect was said to have been a parody.

Alfred Kerr, the great theatre critic, arrived at quite a different conclusion. In his periodical *Pan* he wrote enthusiastically about the performance:

'*Pierrot Lunaire* . . . what it allowed us to hear appears to me not as the end of music; but as the beginning of a new stage in listening.

'To interpret this last work, which melts into sound the universal feelings and sorrows of the moonlight Harlequin with a grandiose, many-sided, devious yet exact picture full of sobs, shrillness, brooding and depression;—to interpret this the actress Zehme stood as the speaker. Certainly she did not give a perfect performance; much was amateurish, yet it was all the more shattering than what a more accomplished actress could have achieved; unselfishly and unaffectedly she gave all of herself.

'Yes, she even prostituted herself, renouncing all shame (as it should be in art), in an absolute task of precision as a servant of the work.'

Even such an expert on the work as Hermann Scherchen,[1] who partnered her in later performances, spoke of Zehme with a high regard.

The faults with which Marschalk debits her arise from the work itself. Whether we regard them as a weakness or an advantage, they are irrevocably linked to its style, and are even consciously brought into the conception of this whole artistic undertaking.

The exact title of Schoenberg's opus 21 is 'Thrice seven poems from Albert Giraud's *Pierrot Lunaire*', in German translation by Otto Erich Hartleben, for a speaking voice (Sprechstimme), piano, flute (doubling piccolo), clarinet (doubling bass-clarinet), violin (doubling viola) and violoncello ; and he adds in brackets as a subtitle the word 'Melodramas'. The melodrama, a combination of spoken verse or prose and accompanying music, has always been regarded as a problematical form. Neither the old chamber musician from Bohemia, Georg Benda, who practised it in 1750 in North Germany, nor the composers of the twentieth century, such as Richard Strauss and Max Schillings, have been able to infuse it with permanent life. But Schoenberg's new attempt differs from their melo-dramas in one important point. The speaking part of *Pierrot Lunaire* is not only noted down rhythmically as exactly as is usual with sung parts; it was actually written by Schoenberg in note-values, notes with sharps and flats and returns to naturals. In some instances it even moves into real sung sounds. Nevertheless, as he explains in the foreword to the score,

---

[1] German conductor, b. 1891. He has given the first performances of numerous works of Schoenberg, Berg and Webern, and many of the younger composers have studied with him.

Schoenberg desires (apart from a few exceptions) no sung notes, but a spoken melody 'taking into careful account the notated pitch'. He even warns the interpreter against any temptation to fall into a kind of sing-song speech and demands a recognition of the difference between a sung note and a spoken note. He defines the difference thus: the sung note keeps to the level of the note without changing; the spoken note gives it, yet immediately leaves it to fall or rise.

We cannot doubt that Schoenberg anticipated the difficulties which arise from this in actual performance. What artistic motivation may have led him to an attempt in this novel form?

We do not believe, as Hans Mersmann tried to prove, that we are dealing here with a logical continuation of the path taken by the development of the singing voice. Schoenberg certainly did not consider the possibilities of singing as exhausted. Shortly before *Pierrot* he had composed *Herzgewaechse* for coloratura soprano, and shortly afterwards the Four Orchestral Songs opus 22 were written. None of these pieces, as far as vocal writing is concerned, is linked with the experiment in the speaking part of *Pierrot*, and *Herzgewaechse* demands a virtuoso singer.

On the other hand Schoenberg had twice before used 'melodramatic' effects. The first time was very early, in 1901, in the last part of the *Gurrelieder*, where the melodrama *Des Sommerwindes wilde Jagd* ('The Summer Wind's Wild Chase') prepares as a contrast for the powerful finale of the sunrise with its choral canon. The second time was in *Die Glueckliche Hand*, where a six-part chorus uses a toneless whispering. The contrasting effects attempted in both cases prove that Schoenberg was here striving for abnormal artistic forms. But the melodrama of *Pierrot* does not, as an American musical sociologist, Elie Siegmeister, believes, indicate the approach of bourgeois music to complete helplessness. On the contrary, it arose from the wish to compose a given text in a more flexible manner and with a greater wealth of intervals smaller than semitones and ambiguous sounds than a singing voice would have allowed. It makes possible a treatment of the human voice in the same way as that often attempted on the stage by the Symbolist theatre in the years before the first world war. This aimed at a synthesis of the most complete anti-naturalistic stylisation with the strictest musical notation to which one can subject the speaking voice. Artistic intention and realistic effect here serve a double purpose: that of drama and psychology.

How far do the poems used by Schoenberg take part in this form? *Pierrot Lunaire* appeared in French in 1884. Its author was a little-known Belgian, a member of a Brussels literary group which called itself 'Le Parnasse de la Jeune Belgique'. At the time the poems caused a certain stir, though the poet did not occupy any very important place in the Parnassus. But they contained a macabre attractiveness of ironical aestheticism, and they depicted Pierrot, who appears here together with his colleagues from the Italian comedy, against a motley background full of glowing colour, bizarre events, ghostly encounters and horrifying enterprises. (The title rôles of Busoni's *Arlecchino* of 1917 and Stravinsky's *Petrushka* of 1911 also rely on the Commedia dell'arte.)

Giraud's Dandy of 1884 bears the traces of a conceited and blasé decadence common to a certain genre of literature of the late nineteenth century. They are characteristics which are also to be found, albeit on a higher literary and moral level, in the novel of Joris Karl Huysman, *À rebours*. For the psychologist and psychoanalyst the verses are not without attraction. They contain certain sado-masochistic turns, and moods of malaise and perversity. Giraud allows much blood to flow: from the thin breasts of the Madonna, from the Host which becomes Pierrot's heart on the occasion of the Red Mass, from the

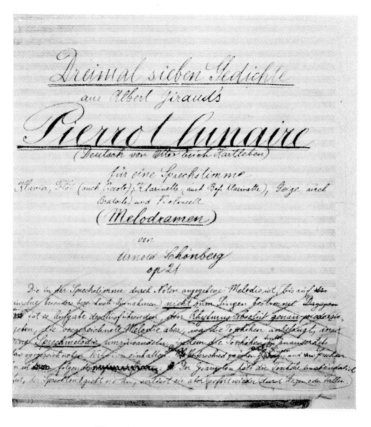

The title page of *Pierrot Lunaire*

Pierrot Lunaire: a performance in Italy in 1924
Arnold Schoenberg (fourth from left), Erika Wagner (in the middle), Alfredo Casella (behind Erika Wagner), members of the Pro Arte Quartet, Eduard Erdmann and flautist Fleury

coffins in which he seeks to find rubies, from the lips of a sick woman who appears behind the strains of a Chopin waltz, in the bodies of poets who are crucified by their verses. There is also an image of blood where Pierrot uses his drill on the bald head of his enemy Cassander in order to smoke tobacco out of his skull.

In an essay André Schaeffner compared the original French version of Giraud's poems with their German counterpart, which Hartleben published about twenty years later. He concluded that the translation is superior to the original, both in literary form and power as well as in taste. For example, in the *Valse de Chopin* Giraud speaks of a 'crachat sanguinolant'—the spitting of blood by a tubercular. Hartleben modifies this crass expression into 'a pale drop of blood on the lips of a sick woman'.

The setting to music of such subjects is characteristic of the late romantic period and of many composers around the turn of the century and in the years before the first world war. Wagner's *Parsifal* contains the seeds of it; but the tendency reached its climax in Richard Strauss's *Salome* and *Elektra*. Yet what in Strauss is described with all the means of naturalism, in Schoenberg takes the form of a highly differentiated and musically stylised psychology. Virgil Thomson spoke with some critical insight, in connection with *Pierrot Lunaire*, of microscopic examinations, of psychological analyses of a given poetic content.

Igor Stravinsky was among the audience of one of the last rehearsals before the Berlin first performance in the autumn of 1912. The Russian Ballet of Sergei Diaghilev was then performing in Berlin, and was giving his *Firebird* and *Petrushka*; the half-completed score of *Sacre du Printemps* accompanied the composer on his travels. Stravinsky reports his impressions of *Pierrot* in the *Chroniques de ma vie*. He was repelled by

E

something which he called 'Beardsleyan aesthetic'. Though this criticism may do little justice to the spirit of Schoenberg's score, the comparison has a certain justification as far as the text is concerned. A symbolism approaching Aubrey Beardsley's and that of Art nouveau forms the basis of Giraud's poems and their translation by Hartleben.

The verse technique of the poems may well have exercised a special charm on Schoenberg. Giraud-Hartleben used a form of thirteen lines in which the seventh and last repeat the first in the style of a motto. The second line is also repeated as the eighth. Thus a formal scheme results: A-B-C-D——E-F-A-B——G-H-I-K-A. In other words a musical form, the reprise, is translated into poetry.

At that time the problem of form had become a crucial subject of artistic endeavour for Schoenberg. In 1907 and 1908, in the second string quartet and the *Georgelieder*, he had taken that step which he described as 'breaking through the limits of a bygone aesthetic'. All tonality was dispensed with; and dissonance was accorded the same standing as consonance. Thus the two most important forms of classical music, sonata and fugue, were stripped of the tonal tensions which they had carried for hundreds of years. No longer was there any tonic-dominant relationship or centre of gravity in the sense of the traditional cadence. Polyphony, the most essential element in Schoenberg's music, gained a sort of autonomy, being its own law which freed it from the fetters of harmony. The creative results are well known, if not yet analytically clarified. There arose the phenomenon of the diminution of form, which can be clearly seen in the compression of the Small Piano Pieces opus 19 and in the works of Anton von Webern. It produced the athematic style which is the foundation of the mono-drama *Erwartung*.

Compared with these two works, *Pierrot Lunaire* is the first attempt to go beyond this development. Consciously and even programmatically Schoenberg here employs a musical style of complete tonal and harmonic freedom in a series of traditional formal shapes. With the full force of his invention and experience as a composer he fills these with a totally new world of sound.

If there was anything new about the Giraud-Hartleben poems it was the combination of strictness of form and freedom of content. However great the difference in level between the poems and Schoenberg's music, nevertheless in this synthesis they found some answering echo in him. According to his own confession his relationship to the text was often purely impressionistic. He once described how in the case of Schubert Lieder which he knew by heart, he nevertheless remained hazy about the events described in the text. This may be the key to the peculiar unconcern vis-à-vis forms, and even the occasional arbitrary choice of texts, which strikes us in his vocal works.

The *Pierrot* cycle consists of three parts, with seven miniature poems in each. Its total length is about half an hour, so that each poem takes approximately eighty-five seconds. Among it are aphoristic, ghostly, fleeting numbers such as the *Galgenlied*, the twelfth of the cycle, which takes thirteen seconds, and broadly conceived ones like No. 5, the *Valse de Chopin*, or the Passacaglia *Nacht*, which as No. 8 introduces the second part.

This Passacaglia, the most sombre Nocturne of the cycle, is a compendium of examples of thematic and motivic working. The uncompromising responsibility for every single note, which increasingly characterises Schoenberg's music with his growing maturity, can be clearly seen in this piece. The way in which a closely worked three-part canon is developed from the very first bars out of the three-note motif E-G-E-flat, and moreover compresses these three notes into chords, the way in which the distance of a semitone between the two lower notes of the motif is developed further into a chromatic descent of six notes—this alone is a miniature masterpiece of what Schoenberg once called the form of 'developing variation'. And this is only the beginning. The three-note motif appears in a hundred variants, diminished in quaver and crotchet movement, in three-part chords with a fixed rhythmical arrangement, in contrapuntal and canonic forms, and mirrored in its retrograde inversion. Simultaneously the chromatic lines run upwards and downwards, the movement increases, the dynamics move from a barely audible *ppp* to *fff*; finally the dramatically heightened activity ceases abruptly, and the quiet bass of the beginning is reached once more. But all this does not exist for its own formal sake; it succeeds in clarifying and heightening the sinister picture conjured up by the text, of sombre black giant moths which kill the rays of the sun, and descend as invisible monsters earthwards from the sky on heavy wings into the hearts of men. The American writer James Huneker, deeply impressed and disturbed, called this Passacaglia a vision of pre-historic night; it mingles bass clarinet, cello and piano only in extraordinary sounds.

Schoenberg reveals a highly skilled contrapuntal technique in the eighteenth piece, *Mondfleck*. The text shows Pierrot walking on a warm evening, with a white spot from the bright moon on the back of his black frock-coat. Since he is vain, and in addition is out for adventure, something worries him about his clothes. He inspects himself and finds the moon spot. He rubs at what he believes to be a plaster spot, but cannot get it off, and goes on rubbing it into the early morning.

Schoenberg takes a moment from this curious episode which attracts his musical imagination, the point where Pierrot looks round at himself and discovers the spot on his back. That a man should be able to see his own back is an odd situation.

In a different form it had already inspired Schoenberg. Among the pictures which he painted in 1907 and 1910 are several self-portraits. One of them shows him from behind walking up a mountain. In order to paint it, Schoenberg had to make studies in the mirror. He observed so accurately that the portrait reflects the way he held himself and the back of his head with its round tonsure-like bald patch.

Here he uses the same technique of the mirror-picture in a musical form. The whole piece is a double mirror or crab canon between the piccolo and clarinet on the one hand, and the violin and cello on the other. That means that the four parts, linked in pairs, run forward to a certain point and then backwards. The point where the movement runs through the mirror lies between the words of the text 'richtig' and 'einen weissen Fleck' (a white spot). Besides the content of the poems Giraud's method of repetitions of lines may well have inspired Schoenberg's imagination. Simultaneously with the mirror movement of the wind and strings there is a piano accompaniment in fugue but not in a mirror form.

Canonic and fugal writing of this kind, which reminds one of the music of the Netherlands polyphonists of the fifteenth and sixteenth centuries, can also be found in other pieces in the cycle, especially in the second part. Thus *Parodie*, which precedes *Mondfleck*, has at its beginning a canon in inversion between viola and clarinet, to which, as a third part, the speaking voice is added, imitating the viola; and later the imitation is repeated, this time between speaking voice and piccolo.

Besides these purely contrapuntal forms which arise from the events in the text, this unusually complex score contains others which are homophonic, such as *Serenade*, which is played in a slow waltz rhythm with a virtuoso cello part whose cantilenas and cadenzas are almost entirely accompanied by chords or figurations on the piano. In a similar way No. 9, the *Gebet an Pierrot*, combines flute, clarinet, and piano, and No. 2, *Colombine*, flute, clarinet, violin, and piano. No. 7, *Der kranke Mond*, is a pure concertante piece in which a soft flute alone accompanies the widely ranging Sprechstimme.

Instrumental colour is one of the strongest means of contrast in *Pierrot Lunaire*—different in each piece and tried out in ever new combinations. The five players use eight instruments; the violin doubles viola, the flute piccolo, and the clarinet bass clarinet. Schoenberg's instrumentation is peculiar in its ability to distil the essence of the tone-colour belonging to each individual instrument. While classical and romantic orchestration are dominated by the wish to find a common denominator in sound and invariably to achieve the greatest blend of tone-colour (even if occasionally colour contrasts are employed as dissonances, so to speak), Schoenberg's sound palette is based on emphatic contrasts. One could say that in *Pierrot* the colour extremes of each instrument are discovered anew. This is as true for the wind as for the string instruments, and also for the piano, the predominating instrument of the work. The balance of instrumental colour is distributed as follows: the piano appears in seventeen pieces, the clarinet and cello in fourteen each, the violin and flute in twelve each, the piccolo in seven, the bass clarinet in six and the viola in five.

Because of the predominant sound of the piano, the need to differentiate it clearly arises. From the most closely woven polyphony to the simplest broken chords, the piano parts for each individual piece are differently heard and used, and range from the fullest of sounds to simple part-writing, from soloistic predominance to a basic accompanimental function.

Only in the last piece, *O alter Duft*, do all eight instrumental colours appear. It is the simplest example of a predominantly homophonic song in varied strophes. But not every strophe of the poem corresponds to one in the composition. By constantly changing the periods there are surprises from bar to bar; the simple main theme appears diminished, inverted, in three-

part chords, varied in figuration and in a canon between its own diminution and its inversion. The speaking part, which in the first bar more or less speaks in unison with the piano, does the same thing in the fourteenth bar in canon with the piano. The impression of simplicity is strengthened by presenting the theme in thirds. It is in E major, with a 6/4 chord in the third and sixteenth bars. At the end there is a varied major cadence. The E in the bass with which the piano ends produces in a sense a resolution of the dissonance; since it was preceded by an augmented triad E flat, G, B natural, so the human ear has the understandable weakness to add the missing notes G sharp and B natural to the E.

The simplicity of this last piece is a result of the text. In Hartleben's version it says 'A happy wish makes me aspire to joys which I long despised'. Perhaps these despised joys then, in this critical stage of Schoenberg's development, included tonality, triads and consonances? Much later in an essay, *On revient toujours*, Schoenberg discussed the tonal compositions of his American years. The last of the 'Pierrot' melodramas, and the mention in its text of 'happy wishes', may remind us of these later utterances of Schoenberg's.

Pierrot Lunaire is one of the representative works of the twentieth century, as much as Pablo Picasso's *Man with the Guitar* or James Joyce's *Ulysses*. As a creative effort in a single consistent style, as an artistic phenomenon, it stands alone even among Schoenberg's compositions. The era of 1912, the sunset of a long epoch of peaceful construction in Central Europe, found an unmistakable expression in it.

In the two succeeding years, until the outbreak of the first world war, Schoenberg composed only one more work: the four orchestral songs opus 22 to poems of Rainer Maria Rilke and Ernest Dowson (in a translation by Stefan George). They are written for contralto voice and varied, sometimes very unusual, instrumental forces. In style they widen the polyphony achieved in *Pierrot* to a polyharmony in which groups of chords are set against single parts. The harmony here is much thicker and more massive than in the two works for the stage; the forms are freer than in the preceding opus, yet still clearly bound by tradition. The vocal part is written with the lightness and naturalness of the spoken word, and completely adapts itself to the curious dreamlike quality of the text.

These last pre-war years, however, were full of many other events. In the autumn of 1912 *Arnold Schoenberg*, a symposium, was published by R. Piper in Munich; it included contributions from his pupils and friends about the varied manifestations of his genius, reproductions of some of his paintings, musical examples, a portrait and a list of the more important dates in his life. In the same year the *Blaue Reiter* was also published by Piper—this great manifesto of a new revolutionary artistic movement, among whose collaborators Schoenberg also took part. As a result larger circles began to learn of his existence, and above all people outside Austria and Germany began to take note of the much-discussed experimental composer. In 1912 *Pelleas und Melisande* was heard in Amsterdam, and on 3 September Sir Henry Wood performed the Orchestral Pieces opus 16 for the first time. In 1912, also, Schoenberg orchestrated songs by Schubert, Beethoven (*Adelaide*) and Carl Loewe (*Der Noeck*).

Among the many private pupils who had learnt of Schoenberg through the publication of the *Harmonielehre* there had
been since 1911 a member of the inner Bayreuth circle: Count
Gilbert Gravina, the grandson of Hans von Bülow and
Cosima. He remained with Schoenberg till 1914.

In February of 1913 Franz Schreker and the Vienna Philharmonic Chorus performed for the first time the mammoth
score of the *Gurrelieder*. The performance, which had been
splendidly prepared and included first-class soloists, was a
tremendous success. Yet even though a wider audience was
ready to accept Schoenberg's style of 1900, few knew what
to make of the more recent works of this composer and his
pupils which were given in another concert on 31 March 1913.
This resulted in an uproar of which the musical history of
Vienna has no similar example, ending in a fight and leading
to a much-discussed lawsuit. That even in Berlin the increasing
international successes of Schoenberg were watched with
dislike was shown by the open letter of a now-forgotten critic
after the Berlin première of the Three Piano Pieces opus 11.
(The pianist Richard Buhlig played them at a solo piano
recital.) From the letter we learn that among the audience
who applauded were Ferruccio Busoni and his pupils, and that
Alfred Kerr with his 'Pan' circle continued to support Schoenberg.

Between the completion of opus 22 (about New Year 1915)
and the composition of the next work, the Five Piano Pieces
opus 23, there is an interval of more than eight years during
which Schoenberg did not write down a complete work. And
yet these eight years contained the decisive development of his
musical growth. His path, after the breaking of all traditional
shackles, led to new constructive ideas which were to influence
the future of world music for generations.

THE INTERLUDE

At the moment when Schoenberg's fame began to spread abroad, when London, Amsterdam and St Petersburg had learnt to know him and his works by repeated performances, the era ended which had made this strong blossoming of new artistic ideas in the West possible. The first world war destroyed many links of European collaboration for a considerable time; it decimated a generation whose best spirits had been receptive to new ideas. It erected spiritual barriers which it took a decade to remove.

At the outbreak of war Schoenberg was passing through Berlin, and there he remained for the moment. At the beginning of 1915 he wrote the text of part of his great projected oratorio, the scherzo-like second section, which he called the 'Totentanz der Prinzipien', and then the libretto of the third movement, which was published under the title of *Die Jakobsleiter*, but the music of which remained a sketch until it was continued in 1945. Schoenberg was twice a soldier in the Austrian army, from December 1915 to September 1916, and again from July to October 1917. Of his military days we know only that Schoenberg with his peculiar radicalism attempted to vanish into total anonymity, and be nothing but a soldier. It is reported that he found it displeasing to be questioned about musical matters. But on the occasion of a company celebration he had to comply with a demand for a composition; to the astonishment of his comrades he wrote the music (according to his own account in the book *Style and Idea*) 'as if he were writing a letter'. This great facility he retained throughout his life; just as *Erwartung* was written down in eighteen days, so one of his late works, the *Survivor from Warsaw*, was completed in a week.

The first sketches for the music of the *Jakobsleiter* stem from the interlude between the two periods of army service. The text of the work has from time to time been appropriated by the theosophists as a cornerstone of their philosophy, since it is based on the idea of reincarnation. It is in fact a philosophical creed, even a religious creed, without however being tied to a definite religion. The leading figure, which Egon Wellesz compares to the Evangelist in the classical oratorio, is the archangel Gabriel, in whom we can recognise Schoenberg himself. He meets many other figures, some singly, some in groups, here one who is struggling or an agitator, a monk or a dying man, there a rationalist, a sceptic, or one of many super-natural creatures.

We know today that in the conception and form of the work Schoenberg was not merely preoccupied in a very personal manner with questions of creed and religion; the score contains the germs of a technique which in the years to follow he was to develop much further.

In 1917 Schoenberg was finally released from military service. Now he started upon a period of teaching within the framework of the teaching institutions, run on the most progressive modern educational principles, which had been founded by Dr Eugenie Schwarzwald in Vienna. These were schools in which the most gifted of the Austrian youth were taught in the spirit of a new tolerant social and humanitarian world citizenship by a comradely community of teachers with modern attitudes. It was a congenial framework for Schoen-berg's artistic 'craft teaching'. The courses were called 'Semin-ary for Composition'; they enabled a growing circle of pupils to enjoy Schoenberg's fascinating personality. Among the pupils of this period were Max Deutsch, Hanns Eisler, Rudolf Kolisch, Erwin Ratz, Josef Rufer, Karl Rankl, Rudolf Serkin, Eduard Steuermann and others. In April 1918 Schoenberg moved to Moedling near Vienna, where from then on he held courses in his house until the Seminar was dissolved in 1920.

Schoenberg had an individual way of teaching which matched his intelligence—this was extraordinarily mobile and always ready for discussion. He did not work systematically and did not keep to a definite scheme, but instead treated each individual pupil as a special case. So he became a colleague to those seeking his instruction; he did not merely correct compositions, but when necessary rewrote a whole piece with his pupil, showing him why it needed changing. The authoritative weight of his knowledge and ability in composition technique frequently resulted in a creative paralysis of his pupils at first. Many never overcame this deadlock; almost without exception it turned out that their talent was insufficient. Others, after a time of paralysis, rediscovered their inner resources and through Schoenberg's teaching were enriched to an extent that was to be decisive for the rest of their lives. Almost every one who came as a pupil to Schoenberg expected something different from what he found. Schoenberg never gave instruction in modern music, and in the analytical courses, which he held first in Moedling and later in Berlin, contemporary works were rarely and only exceptionally studied. He concentrated on the period of the flowering of Western music, from Bach to Brahms. The works of the Viennese classics—Haydn, Mozart and Beethoven—were the centre of all technical, formal, harmonic and aesthetic teaching. Schoenberg always directed his pupils back to their works. Among the older masters, Bach was nearest to him; beside him he considered Handel to be a lesser figure, and Gluck and

Weber meant less to him than the greater masters to whom he felt spiritually related.

About Schoenberg as a teacher much has been written in Austria, Germany and America, but nothing more apt than what Dr Heinrich Jalowetz said in the Schoenberg book which was published in 1912 by Piper: 'A. S. possesses the two basic abilities of every genius and thus of every teacher of genius: on the one hand the force of naïve perception which can do without the help of tradition and which forces him to re-formulate everything, from the smallest everyday matters of life to the highest human and artistic questions and to make it live anew; on the other hand the power of communicating his personal evaluation of these matters in a convincing way. Out of these two basic forces of his personality derives the miracle of his way of teaching, his unique effect on his pupils. All the artistic rules which seem dry in old text-books and from the lips of bad teachers appear in his lessons to have been born at that moment from an immediate perception, or else they suddenly appear in a new light which brings them to life, quite apart from the totally new insight which his personal approach always opens up. In this manner every stage of his teaching becomes an experience for his pupil, and really sinks into his personality. In this independent treatment of the material he strictly demands the most complete artistic cleanness, so that the pupil comes to regard an unmotivated progression as a fault. Thus he aims at the growth of a sense of "musical clean-ness", which in due course will recognise without the help of a book of rules what is true and what is false.'

From this collaboration with his pupils the wish arose to get to know in sound some of the controversial modern works which had been debated during these discussions. To meet these wishes Schoenberg invented something not previously done. In the spring of 1918 he conducted ten public rehearsals of his chamber symphony, which were not however followed by a performance; they served the purpose of familiarising a circle of people with the score more thoroughly than would have been possible in the study without comparison with the actual sound of the music.

This form of educational rehearsal became a main theme of the 'Verein fuer musikalische Privatauffuehrungen' (Society for Private Musical Performances) which was founded in Vienna immediately after the armistice in November 1918. Schoenberg was chosen as President and Alban Berg drew up its statutes. Three main points were mentioned as essential for the education of members: clear, well-prepared performances; frequent repetitions; exclusion of the public. Only members were allowed into the Sunday performances; they had to show a membership card with a photograph. Members undertook neither to applaud nor to show their displeasure and to publish nothing about the works and their performances (naturally the Press was also excluded from the concerts). The number of compositions which were performed by this society is vast: in the first season, 1918-1919, twenty-six concerts were given, and forty-five works received a total of ninety-five performances. During the third year the number rose to 226. Among them not only the most radical modern works were represented: forty-two little-known works by Max Reger were given, and also compositions by Debussy, Mahler, Pfitzner, Stravinsky, Suk and Webern.

The activities of the society started in the hall of the Schwarzwald schools, where Schoenberg had begun his seminar in 1918, and also in the hall of the Kaufmaennischer Verein. Later the society moved to the small Musikverein-und Konzerthaussaal. In 1921 the society had to be liquidated as the result of the decline in value of Austrian currency.

The best interpreters took part. Pianists such as Rudolf

Serkin and Eduard Steuermann put their art at the disposal of the society for a long period; the violinist Rudolf Kolisch and the singers Marie Gutheil-Schoder, Felicie Hueni-Mihacsek and Erika Wagner were amongst those taking part. The extremely exact style of performance pursued here clearly and perman- ently exerted its influence on many of the younger musicians. The principle was to rehearse each work to 'its end', which meant rarely less than ten rehearsals. The closest members of Schoenberg's circle, Alban Berg, Erwin Stein, Anton von Webern, directed the rehearsals or acted as 'concert chairman'.

Schoenberg was the soul of this artistic enterprise, to which he dedicated himself exclusively for the whole of 1919 in addition to his teaching post. In 1920 he travelled once more, to Prague, Mannheim and Amsterdam, where he conducted his own works. In June (shortly after he had been elected President of the International Mahler-League) he saw the triumph of two performances of his *Gurrelieder* in the Vienna Staatsoper. From the autumn of 1920 to the beginning of 1921 he lectured on musical theory at Amsterdam, and attracted a large audience of pupils from many countries.

Vienna, to which Schoenberg returned in the spring of 1921, had been in a permanent state of economic crisis since the world war. Austria, once the centre of the all-powerful double monarchy, had become a small country without political importance as the result of the peace treaty of St Germain; it had had to cede its most important industrial areas to the new state of Czechoslovakia, and thus lacked economic viability. Vienna, the glittering capital, had the effect of a too large head on an all too weak body. Yet, in this country that had lost its power, art and culture still continued to flourish and to represent more lasting values which still make Austria internationally famous.

In these first years after the first world war Austria re-established its links with international cultural life much faster than Germany. Above all in France the music of the new Vienna school was not only performed but was much discussed among modern composers. At this time several of these composers travelled on behalf of the French government as cultural ambassadors to Vienna to re-establish that personal contact which had been broken since 1914. Amongst them was Maurice Ravel, whose music figured regularly among the performances of the Verein fuer musikalische Privatauffuehrungen. Darius Milhaud and Francis Poulenc, then the representatives of the young French avant-garde, came to Vienna too, and received the stimulus of the music there with sympathy and understanding. Poulenc liked to speak of a visit to Schoenberg's flat in Moedling, and many photographs taken on this occasion show him with Schoenberg's family, to which Felix Greissle also belonged as a son-in-law.

The political and social changes also had their important effect on intellectual life. Artists who had formerly belonged to the opposition received official commissions. It seemed for a time as if a great wave of progress was to render Vienna the centre of progressive thought and enterprise. Though this appearance did not last for long, its duration was sufficient to provide people such as Karl Kraus, Adolf Loos and Arnold Schoenberg with a wider fame than hitherto. This growing interest in modern music also found support from the world-wide publishing house which handled the most important works of the modern composers—the Universal Edition under Emil Hertzka, its intelligent director. Since 1919 his publishing firm had brought out a house and publicity journal for modern music, the *Musikblaetter des Anbruch* which, besides much that was bad, also stated the case for Mahler, Schoenberg, Schreker and many others among the leaders of modern music. Schoenberg had concluded his first agreement with Universal Edition

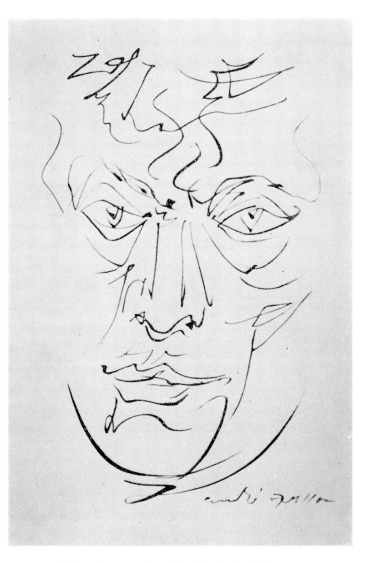

Schoenberg: a drawing by André Masson

Beginning of *Piano Piece* Op. 33a

in 1909, and over the years most of his works were published by them.

Yet by 1921 it still was almost exclusively his older works which were presented to the public. Neither at the Verein fuer musikalische Erstauffuerhrungen nor in the catalogues of the U.-E. did anything of Schoenberg's appear that had been composed later than 1915. Even the pupils and friends of Schoenberg's closest circle did not know how to explain this fact. Some of them had been allowed a glimpse of the sketches for the uncompleted *Jakobsleiter*—the work of the war years 1915-17. After that Schoenberg's inspiration seemed to have dried up.

F

THE LAW

SCHOENBERG spent the summer of 1922 with some pupils in Traunkirchen. During a walk he said to Josef Rufer: 'I have discovered something which will guarantee the supremacy of German music for the next hundred years'. There followed an indication of the 'method of composition with twelve notes'. At the time he had written a number of works in which the method had been consciously used. Schoenberg had not made any of them public: he hesitated for years before he spoke of a discovery and before showing its results, which he knew would take the technique of composition along quite new lines.

The law which Schoenberg discovered is far from being arbitrary. It derives logically and almost automatically from the evolution of our music over the past two hundred years. When in about 1700 Andreas Werckmeister[1] introduced tempered tuning in organs and pianos, i.e. when he divided the octave into twelve mathematically equal parts, an enormous step towards the gradual conquest of nature by the spirit had been taken. As a result of this rationalisation of the tonal system, freedom of modulation and the equality of all chromatic notes were secured as a matter of principle. A logical almost pre-calculated path leads from the 48 Preludes and Fugues of Bach's *Well-Tempered Clavier* through the chromaticism of Wagner's *Tristan* and the harmonic discoveries of Reger, Strauss, Debussy and Mahler to the frontiers of the major and minor tonalities. It seems probable that systems similar to Schoenberg's have been discovered earlier, simul-

[1] German organist, composer and theoretician (1645-1706).

taneously and later by other composers. Priority in this case is of little importance. The Russian Jefim Golyscheff, the Viennese Josef Matthias Hauer,[1] the Franco-American Edgar Varèse[2] arrived at similar conclusions independently of Schoenberg. But the consequences which Schoenberg drew from them for the technique of composition are so wide and comprehensive that they go far beyond the other twelve-note pioneers. It thus suffices to deal with his system alone to understand the others.

The law which is obeyed by all twelve-note disciples, and before which the differences of methods vanish, is this: no note should be repeated before the other eleven notes have been used. (Excepted are immediate rhythmical repetitions, so that for example the first bars of Beethoven's C minor Symphony with their threefold Gs and Fs would be entirely feasible within the framework of a twelve-note composition.) Such sequences of twelve different notes are to be found in old music as far back as the madrigalists of around 1600; Luca Marenzio and Heinrich Schuetz wrote chord sequences which contain all twelve chromatic notes without repetitions. In the *Faust* symphony of Liszt one of the main themes consists of four different broken augmented triads which together make up the chromatic scale. Richard Strauss in his *Zarathustra* of 1896 wrote a fugue theme (*Von der Wissenschaft*) which consists of twelve different notes in succession, and in Reger there occur such frequent ten-, eleven- and occasionally twelve-note sequences that it is already possible to speak of an unconscious obedience to the law of the non-repetition of notes.

The most important factor in Schoenberg's 'method of composition with twelve notes' is the principle of the supremacy of the row (or series). The 'row' (or, as Thomas Mann

[1] b. 1883.
[2] b. 1885.

makes Adrian Leverkuehn call it in his *Doktor Faustus*, the
constellation) is the predetermined sequence of the twelve
notes which is not departed from in the course of the composition. For example, such a row might be: E–D–E flat—B–C–D
flat—A flat-G flat-A-F-G-B flat. It is constantly repeated
during the whole course of a movement, and only its rhythmical structure changes continually, so that the musical
character is constantly changed. Schoenberg only once used
this relatively primitive form of the technique (as he put it),
in the fourth movement of his *Serenade* opus 24, composed in
the early twenties, in the Sonnet no. 217 of Petrarch. The
baritone, accompanied by clarinet, bass clarinet, mandoline,
guitar, violin, viola and cello, in fact sings the same sequence
of twelve notes throughout. Since every line of the poem has
eleven syllables, one note is 'left over', so that each of the first
twelve lines begins with a different note.

Since the same two notes can be linked by different intervals,
(e.g. E-D can be either a major second downwards, or a minor
seventh upwards, or a major ninth downwards, or, according
to circumstances (as often met with in Schoenberg's earlier
works), an even greater interval spanning two octaves and
more), the melodic tension within a row can be very varied.
It is important that technically the intervals between the two
notes are seen as being equivalent, i.e. a fifth upwards is
identical with a fourth downwards, and a minor third upwards
is identical with a major sixth downwards, while the tension
or expressive quality are naturally quite different.

Schoenberg, however, did not content himself with this

'relatively primitive' technique. Just like the old contra-puntalists, he found that a succession of notes (a theme or a row) retains its essential character, irrespective of the side from which it is viewed. Whether the intervals run from top to bottom or the other way round is as unimportant as the question whether they are read from front to back or the other way round. Their character of tension and expression certainly changes basically; but not the nature of their musical structure. Schoenberg himself used the simile of a hat: it is possible to look at it from the front or from the back, from above or below: it remains a hat. Thus with the twelve-note rows, beside their basic form, three other 'perspectives' arise: the inversion, in which the same intervals run upwards instead of downwards and vice versa; the retrograde, in which the row runs backwards; and the retrograde form of the inversion.

For these three 'perspectives' of the row it also holds good, for example, that the step E-D can be taken in one of several ways, as a second, a seventh or a ninth.

Moreover, the rows can be transposed, so that they can appear in twelve different pitches. In brief, the same manifold possibilities exist in this method of composition as in strict counterpoint such as that on whose principles Bach based his *Art of Fugue*.

When Erwin Stein, in his longish essay, 'Neue Formprin-zipien' (New Formal Principles), published the first mature results of this method in 1924, they received a mixed reception. Support came in the main only from the circle around Schoen-berg; others spoke of 'intellectual constructions', of mathe-matical music, of crossword puzzles and worse. True criticism of the method was barely attempted because it is extraordin-arily difficult really to understand and master it. The rules are utterly simple and can be grasped—as Hauer once said—in one hour by any intelligent person, just like the rules of chess. Yet to play chess well requires long practice. But the composer who wants to work according to Schoenberg's twelve-note method must be a good chess player and also an inspired musician—otherwise everything he does remains the same kind of paper music as the polyphonic exercises of an uninspired contrapuntalist. That the law of the row (or series) exercises a strict control of the imagination needs no discussion; it is of course no stricter than that of canonic writing, for example. But that within the twelve-note technique a hundred different types of music can be made, that every temperament, every feeling for melody and sound adapts the rules according to its own needs, is clearly evident today—several decades after the first announcement of this law—from the work of all the musicians who have adopted it. Hauer and Paul von Klenau have, each in his own way, invented a particular kind of twelve-note music which differs from Schoenberg's. Yet from Schoenberg's technique too very varied works arose, such as the late works of Anton von Webern, the violin concerto of Alban Berg (with its use of a Bach chorale in its original harmonisation) and his own works since opus 23.

He himself stated some important facts about the history of his discovery in a letter which he wrote on 3 June 1937 to Nicolas Slonimsky, the Russo-American composer. The 'method of composing with twelve notes' was the subject of many previous attempts, he said there. 'The first step took place in about December 1914 or early in 1915, when I sketched out a symphony whose last part later became the *Jakobsleiter*, but which was never completed. The scherzo of this symphony was built on a theme consisting of twelve notes. . . . As an example of such attempts I might mention the piano pieces opus 23. . . . Contrary to the usual manner of using a motif, I almost used it in the manner of a "basic row of twelve notes". I built other motifs and themes out of it and also accompaniment figures and other chords—but the theme did not consist of twelve notes. . . . Another example of this type of striving towards unity is my *Serenade*. Here you can find many examples of this kind. But the best are the variations, the third movement. The theme consists of a succession of fourteen notes, but only eleven are different, and these fourteen are constantly used throughout the whole of the movement. . . . The fourth movement, "Sonnet", is a real "composition with twelve notes". The technique here is relatively primitive, since it was one of the first works to be written strictly within this method, though not the first—those were some of the movements of the piano suite which I composed in the autumn of 1921. Here I suddenly became conscious of the true importance of my aim: unity and regularity which had led me subconsciously along this path. . . .'

These were the five piano pieces opus 23, as Stein makes clear in the aforementioned essay on Schoenberg's method; Schoenberg himself had mentioned the third one to him as a key example. The pieces are very varied in their formal and technical aspects. According to Stein's analysis, the first is a three-part invention, the second a sonata-form-like movement with a development; both are formally variations, in a wider, modern sense. The other pieces stand on an even higher level of constructional technique. 'There is', Stein writes, 'scarcely one note in the (third) piece which is not simultaneously part of several forms of the basic idea, and is thus open to various interpretations.' The fifth piece, a waltz, uses the continual repetition of a row of twelve notes: C sharp-A-B-E-A flat-E flat-B flat-D-E-E flat-C-F. This is a similar technique to that which we find in the Petrarch Sonnet in the *Serenade*. In this opus 24, which is linked to the light-hearted Viennese tradition, Schoenberg tries to apply the new compositional techniques to a range of older forms like the minuet and the march. In the

whole work it becomes clear that Schoenberg desires to carry
over twelve-note principles into every aspect of composition
including the vertical one, i.e. into chords and accompanying
figures. The sixth movement, the 'Lied', actually in 'song'
(ABA) form, has a theme of eighteen notes, in which all the
twelve chromatic notes appear, and six of them come twice.
The first phrase of the theme consists of

five notes: in the accompaniment appear the other seven that
make up a twelve-note row.

The *Serenade* is peculiar in that its complexity from the point
of view of compositional technique never consciously strikes
the listener. He is diverted in this witty gay work by its fire-
engine noises (in the dance scene), its potpourri-like improvisa-
tions (in the final march), and its Mediterranean chirping sounds
evoked by guitar and mandolin. It is not until the score is
examined that the amount of artistic craftsmanship and
sovereign technique employed becomes apparent.

Opus 23 and 24 are works of the early twenties, when
Schoenberg began work again on the *Jakobsleiter*; as the first
results of the new principle of composition, they are of outstanding importance in Schoenberg's work. They were
followed—also between 1921 and 1924—by two works in
which Schoenberg uses the system, or rather the method, with
almost academic strictness: the Suite for Piano opus 25 and the
Wind Quintet opus 26. Artistically these belong to the most
abstract, most 'brittle' of Schoenberg's compositions and are
extraordinarily difficult to understand. But from the technical
point of view they are a real compendium of the new possi-

bilities; they are the classical works of the twelve-note technique.

The piano suite opus 25 keeps basically to classical forms such as had already been used in the two preceding works. Its six movements are Prelude, Gavotte, Musette, Intermezzo, Minuet, and Gigue. Here for the first time a single row provides constructional material for the whole work: it is the twelve-note row E-F-G-D flat-G flat-E flat-A flat-D-B-C-A-B flat. These notes are presented in three groups of four notes, each of which also appears in its various 'perspectives'— inversion, retrograde and retrograde inversion. To this must be added the transposition of all these forms to the interval of the tritone.

However important it is for the understanding of this music to make clear to oneself its construction, its serial technique (that is to say the 'conditioning' which arises from the predetermined row), nevertheless one will not fathom its essence by this means. The twelve-note method, like the highly original piano writing of this opus 25, is only a means of expressing a certain musical state. The individuality lies behind the notes. Nothing would be more wrong or contrary to Schoenberg's wishes than a one-sided stress on technical analysis. Just like any other kind of music, twelve-note music has to be grasped by its musical character; however perfectly constructed, if inspiration is missing it is like a 'tinkling cymbal'. One can learn to write with twelve notes as mechanically as learning to write canons; it becomes music only when a creative personality uses it.

The same is true of the wind quintet, which, like the piano suite, was written in 1924. In its four movements (Allegro, Scherzo, Adagio and Rondo) it closely approaches the character of the classical sonata, even to the extent of a fifth-relationship between the theme and its answer. The row is constructed in such a way that its second half is almost exactly the same as its first half transposed up a fifth.

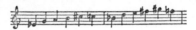

In this first movement we find a strict classical sonata form, with main and subsidiary themes, development, recapitulation, coda, etc., in which the development is on a large scale, as is usual with Schoenberg. The work, which lasts almost an hour, is one of the longest that Schoenberg ever wrote. With it he gained complete technical mastery of the new law. Though uncommonly well written for wind, it is of exorbitant difficulty. The horn part, above all, presupposes a mastery of the instrument in its lowest and highest registers which would be quite enough work for two players. The contrapuntal working-out is more complicated than any since *Pierrot Lunaire*. The Rondo in particular which, because of its rhythmic intelligibility, is the most approachable movement of this opus 26, is a real compendium of contrapuntal mastery and art.

When the quintet was first performed in Vienna in 1924 on the occasion of the Viennese Theatre and Music Exhibition, it was conducted by Anton Webern. Even to Schoenberg's most intimate pupils and followers, it presented a sphinx-like appearance—a riddle one could hardly hope to solve. It belongs to those works which remained almost unperformed until it was revived in 1946. The first performance in Berlin by the wind players of the Staatskapelle brought acclamation; it has since remained in the repertory of this excellent ensemble.

With opus 25 and 26 Schoenberg parted from the town which had been the arena of his early days, and of his hardest battles for recognition. What his native town had denied him

Berlin was to offer. But in Vienna a steadily growing circle of friends revered him, and on his fiftieth birthday a special issue of *Anbruch* appeared containing seventy-four pages with contributions from composers such as Alban Berg, Anton Webern, Hanns Eisler, Franz Schreker, Alfredo Casella and G. F. Malipiero; interpreters including Marya Freund, Marie Gutheil-Schoder, Erika Wagner, Rudolf Kolisch, Arthur Schnabel, Hermann Scherchen and Fritz Stiedry; critics such as Paul Bekker and Adolf Weissmann; theoreticians such as Erwin Stein. But simultaneously he was called to take over the composition class at the Berlin Academy which had fallen vacant through the death of Busoni.

With it there began a new section of Schoenberg's life, which brought some marks of international recognition, at least as a leading composition teacher. His personal life also was affected by fate in the early twenties. In 1923 he lost his wife Mathilde, the sister of Zemlinsky, who had borne him two children. In 1924 he married Gertrud Kolisch, the sister of the violinist Rudolf Kolisch, one of his most faithful pupils and most brilliant interpreters.

In Vienna he left behind a circle of devoted supporters, a group of pupils, some of whom were to follow him to Berlin, and a large number of opponents, who were all the more pleased to see him depart since his successes were growing.

THE BERLIN YEARS

AFTER THE FIRST WORLD WAR Germany, even more than Austria, had become a witches' cauldron of vanishing values. The collapse of the Hohenzollerns, the total decay of the currency, resulting in the mark falling to a billionth of its gold value, the dispossession of the middle classes arising from this —all these were reflected in the anarchistic, chaotic and incoherent intellectual life. But this country possessed one thing—a spiritually revolutionary youth, open to any reform, prepared for any experiment. It was a time above all for new art, new poets, new music and new theatrical experiments. Berlin became the centre of this *ars nova*, not only for Germany but for all Europe. A phalanx of new artists and scientists, who had come to the fore as a result of the fall of the more conservative powers, created an atmosphere of intellectual activity such as had been known before only in Paris. From 1924 onwards post-war Germany began to recover economically. A new material stability, the result of a currency experiment in the grand manner which had been introduced overnight, gave increased security to cultural activities.

As a musical and theatrical centre Berlin had become an international world attraction soon after 1919. Its two opera houses, the Staatsoper Unter Den Linden and the Charlottenburger Opera House, were among the foremost in Europe. The Berlin Philharmonic Orchestra, which since the death of Arthur Nikisch had been conducted by Wilhelm Furtwangler, competed with the Staatskapelle in brilliant performances of classical music. And since the young Erich Kleiber reigned at the Unter Den Linden as General Musical Director, both orchestras showed themselves more willing to undertake modern productions than hitherto. A most active local group of the International Society for Contemporary Music and also the Novembergruppe, an intellectual society founded in 1918 by painters and writers, supported the new music. Since 1920 a review, *Melos*, founded by Hermann Scherchen, had acted as the spearhead for modern composition.

The Prussian State Academy of Arts was the most important publicly supported institute for the teaching of the arts. The State Academy of Music was one of its branches, and out of this the so-called department for musical composition or academic master classes had grown as an independent organism. Founded in 1833, the school had three master classes, which in 1924 were directed by Busoni, Hans Pfitzner and Georg Schumann. Schoenberg took over the class which had become vacant through Busoni's early death.

He arrived in Berlin in September of 1925, and first took an apartment at the Steinplatz, later in the Westend, and finally in the Nuernberger Strasse. The change which Schoenberg's living conditions had undergone were also reflected in his external attitude. In Vienna, in the years of struggle and privation, he had developed some characteristics which had fenced him off from the world. He was regarded as exclusive in his circle of friends, distrustful, easily irritated, and for these reasons a kind of hermit. This antipathy from many sides was compensated for by the faithful and devoted support accorded to him by his pupils and followers, by their faith in him which at times seemed to regard any criticism of their master as blasphemy. 'To Arnold Schoenberg with supreme veneration' —this was the dedication which his pupils inscribed in the book which had appeared in 1912 in the Piper-Verlag. In these years in Vienna Schoenberg's life had been a constant battle against all sorts of difficulties, against material privations and against defamatory campaigns on the artistic and intellectual level. The joint effects of material difficulties, self-defence, struggle for existence and veneration by his pupils thus resulted in a unique atmosphere; and it was not easy for the novice to find his place in the hierarchical circle round this man.

Yet already about 1924 the atmosphere around Schoenberg became easier. With increasing recognition he became more open to the world, and greater material independence caused him to emerge more and more from his hermit's abode at Moedling and to participate in the life of Vienna. Schoenberg then found a style of life appropriate to his standing. And when he arrived in Berlin he left many things behind in Vienna which had hitherto inhibited his character.

Berlin in no way received him with open arms; but, in spite of sharp opposition at times, here there were none of the petty intrigues and backbiting, none of the local small-mindedness that in Vienna had continually pressed on Schoenberg and his like. The tone of artistic argument was more factual here. The bitter, cunning enmity was missing; but also missing was the boundless adoration of a small circle of disciples.

Even music criticism in Berlin was more progressive than in Vienna; such men as Walter Schrenk of the *Deutsche Allgemeine Zeitung*, Siegmund Pisling of the *Acht-Uhr Abendblatt* and Adolf Weissmann of the *B.Z. am Mittag* could within certain limits be regarded as friends of modern music.

Moreover Franz Schreker, a true personal friend, possessed both position and influence in the capital. Since 1920 he had been director of the Hochschule fuer Musik, a sister insitute to the Composition School of the Academy of Arts.

The seat of the latter was a building on the Pariser Platz, in the most aristocratic and architecturally most beautiful part of

Berlin, opposite the French Embassy, between the Hotel Adlon and the Bluecherpalais, in which the American Embassy had its seat. Here the widest of Berlin's avenues, Unter Den Linden, met the Brandenburger Tor, which in turn led to the park of the Tiergarten. Max Liebermann, the great leader of German impressionism, then already nearing eighty, was president of the Academy of Arts; his successor under Hitler was to be the composer Max von Schillings, who enjoys the doubtful fame of having been among those responsible for Schoenberg's and Schreker's dismissal from the Prussian Civil Service in 1933. But in general no instruction was given in the Akademie. Schoenberg had always preferred to collect his pupils together in his private apartment, and he retained this habit here too.

Some of his youngest pupils followed Schoenberg from Vienna to Berlin, such as Winfried Zillig, the eminently gifted Bavarian composer and conductor. But most of those who came to Schoenberg were new. Among those taking instruction in the first year we find the Spaniard Roberto Gerhard, Walter Goehr, who now lives in London, Walter Gronostay (later to become a successful composer for radio, who died in 1936), Peter Schacht, who was killed in the 1939-45 war, the American Adolphe Weiss, a composer and outstanding bassoonist, who lives in Los Angeles, and Joseph Zmigrod, who has become well known under the name of Allan Gray.

It soon proved necessary to lay down certain disciplines for the Academy pupils who were to be introduced by Schoenberg to the higher reaches of composition; Schoenberg took these for granted but did not wish to teach them himself. An old-established member of the circle, Josef Rufer, who had followed the master from Vienna, took over this job. Nominally Rufer figured among the pupils at the Academy, but in fact he was assistant to Schoenberg. With the exception of Zillig, he instructed the others in harmony, counterpoint and form, and to the present day he has continued to teach in the tradition of Schoenberg's methods in Berlin.[1]

To the above-named pupils others were added in the next few years: Norbert von Hannenheim, a highly gifted German from Transylvania with an unstable personality, Charilaos Perpessa, a Greek from Leipzig, Erich Schmid (a Swiss who is now conductor at Zürich Radio), and Niko Skalkottas, a Greek. Among the more or less transitory or occasional pupils of the later years should also be mentioned the Americans Marc Blitzstein and Henry Cowell, and also Rudolf Goehr (a brother of Walter) and Fred Walter.

Relations between teacher and pupils were easy. There were no regular examinations, no university degrees. Concerts of the work of pupils were given at certain irregular intervals, more or less every year. Usually these were of chamber music, in the hall of the Academy at the Pariser Platz; once a concert was given at the Singakademie am Kastanenwaeldchen in order to perform works which needed a larger number of players. On these occasions the best Berlin chamber musicians performed the works of almost all of Schoenberg's pupils of the younger generation for the first time, as well as some of Schoenberg's works.

December 1925 brought an important event for the friends of modern music in Berlin. Erich Kleiber conducted the world première of *Wozzeck* by Alban Berg in the Staatsoper in the Unter Den Linden. It was a performance of unforgettable dramatic and musical tension; Leo Schuetzendorf in the title rôle acted and sang as realistically as did Sigrid Johannsen in the part of Marie; Ludwig Hoerth produced in a non-realistic

---

[1] He wrote the principal explanation of Schoenberg's method, *Composition with Twelve Notes* (Berlin 1952—English translation, Rockliff, London 1954).

The 1957 Zürich performance of *Moses und Aron*

Baur

Design by Paul Haferüng for *Moses und Aron*

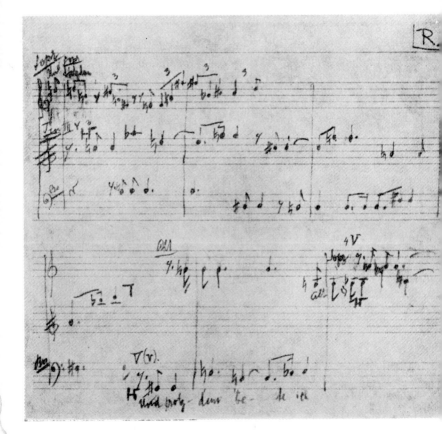

The beginning of the second of the *Modern Psalms*

A sketch for the first of the *Modern Psalms*
(because of the weakness of his eyes, Schoenberg in his last
years wrote on music paper which was specially made for him)

manner. The performance, which was attended by Berg and Schoenberg, was very widely acclaimed in the international press; the work was much opposed by the more conservative section of the public and the critics, but it was generally accepted as a definite landmark. In its dimensions it was the largest creative product to come from the Schoenbergian school. Its importance then was more guessed at than understood. Yet *Wozzeck* remained in the repertory of the Unter den Linden Opera House, and was soon to appear on many other German stages. It is dedicated to Alma Mahler,[1] who was responsible for its publication and thus its wider distribution by *Universal Edition*; she now lives in Los Angeles not far from the house Schoenberg inhabited before his death.

In 1925 Schoenberg returned to a form of composition which he had neglected since opus 13 (*Friede auf Erden*) of 1907. He wrote choral music. In applying the twelve-note-row technique to vocal music and especially to music for *a cappella* chorus, he took an important step into a hitherto totally unexplored area of composition. Of the four pieces for mixed choir opus 27, three are unaccompanied; the fourth, *Der Wunsch des Liebhabers*, uses mandoline, clarinet, violin and cello for the accompaniment to emphasise its serenade-like character. The text of the first and second choruses are Schoenberg's own. Their philosophical lyricism is comparable to that of *Jakobsleiter* or *Glueckliche Hand*; the lines, written in a rhythmically lively prose, speak of self-analysis and painful acknowledgement of fate. 'Du musst an den Geist glauben! Unmittelbar, gefuehllos und selbstlos' ('You must believe in the Spirit! immediately, without feeling or self'). The second song is entitled *Du sollst nicht, du musst!* ('You should not, you must!').

The other two pieces are based on poems from Hans

---

[1] Widow of the composer, and mother of Manon Gropius, in whose memory Berg wrote his violin concerto.

Bethge's *Chinese Flute*, an anthology of oriental poems, which was also used by Gustav Mahler in his *Lied von der Erde*. *Mond und Menschen*, the third of the choruses, constitutes a transition from the philosophical lyricism of the first two to the pure poetry of the fourth, which effectively concludes the work with a kind of small cantata. The varying character of the texts is clearly reflected in the music; the first two are imitative, the first being a canon in contrary motion; the second is also a canon, the third highly contrapuntal. Only the fourth is guided by nothing but sound. The twelve-note row chosen here, D-flat-E-flat-B-flat-G-flat-A-flat-E-B-C-D-A-F-G, in some of its sub-divisions makes pseudo-tonal lines and chords possible. It is employed in these subdivisions throughout the piece and in such a manner that the notes 1 to 5 and 8 to 12 appear as independent motifs, while the middle of the row, the notes 6 and 7, which are heard as an interval, provide an atmospheric background. In the basic form of the row this is a fifth (or when necessary a fourth) E-B; but already in the second bar the basic idea uses one of its changes of 'perspective', the retrograde inversion, and moreover is transposed a fifth lower. In this changed form the fifth or fourth in the middle of the row appears as the interval E flat-A flat. And these two intervals, E-B and E-flat-A-flat, dominate the structure of the whole, mainly homophonic choral movement, in which the mandoline and cello act as the main support of these lightly hovering fifth- and fourth-sounds, which are incessantly repeated like the call of a bird.

Sehr leicht und zart im Ausdruck und Tempo

One recognises from this example what freedom even the prohibition of repetitions allows. Here the two notes which together form the fifth and the middle of the row lead an independent existence. Their repetition has a rhythmical significance and thus no thematic consequences. Also the use of inversion, retrograde and retrograde inversion represents a relaxation of the logical prohibition of repetitions, since these forms of the row necessarily present different arrangements of the twelve notes.

The peculiar, slightly strange charm of the *Wunsch des Liebhabers* is in the use of pseudo-tonal sounds, which are 'consonant' in the traditional sense. These apparently exert a sort of tonal function on one another. As a result the ear constantly expects a functional continuation of what is only the result of a special construction of the row. Similarly Josef Matthias Hauer used chord-sequences which can be understood as a continually modulating extension of tonality, although they keep strictly to the twelve-note law.

During these years of teaching in Berlin a second choral work was written, the three Satires for mixed chorus, opus 28. The text is again Schoenberg's own. These brought him much enmity, for here war is declared without any inhibition on many features of modern music which differ from Schoenberg's. The neo-classicists, the folklorists, and all the other 'ists' are assailed, and in case anyone should not understand the texts, the score contains a foreword which leaves no doubt about this. Two of the satires are again unaccompanied; one is accompanied by viola, cello and piano. To demonstrate that twelve-note music is no playground for those who want to take things easy, Schoenberg added to the work a bundle of complicated canons which make do with completely tonal means. Here there can already be seen what became evident later in some of the works of the American period: the importance of the new strict method of composition even for works not based on twelve-note rows.

The year ended with a performance of the F sharp minor quartet, an event which Schoenberg regarded as a particularly happy one. 'It was a pleasure to hear the notes performed not only with the right expression, but to hear them also with the right intonation and stress', he wrote on 3 June 1926 in the score of the soprano soloist, Margot Hinnenberg-Lefèbre.[1] That same month the International Society for Contemporary Music performed the wind quintet at its Zürich festival.

In 1926 and 1927, besides an extensive teaching activity, two important chamber works of a purely instrumental character saw the light of day—the suite opus 29 and the third string quartet. The suite is written for an unusual ensemble: E flat clarinet, B flat clarinet, bass clarinet, string trio and piano. Its four movements, Overture, Tanzschritte (Dance Steps), Langsam and Gigue, show, in a manner similar to that of the wind quintet, a use of the twelve-note technique in broad flowing forms of a traditional kind. The slow movement consists of variations on a romantic, completely tonal theme, Silcher's song *Aennchen von Tharau*.

The four movements of the third string quartet opus 30 are similarly classical in their construction. In the growth of the musical language the path from the first quartet (1905) through the second (1908) to the third is vast and highly symptomatic of Schoenberg's musical development. Yet as far as personal style is concerned the three scores have much in common. In the form the return to tradition is unmistakable. In this sense the main works of the twenties, the *Serenade*, wind quintet, suite and third quartet, constitute a classical period in Schoenberg's creative activity in which, nevertheless, the link with

---

[1] A singer well known for her performances of modern works, particularly those of Schoenberg. She is married to H. H. Stuckenschmidt.

tradition is achieved not through outward gestures of melody and harmony, but through a strict if unusually expanded use of classical forms.

If one analyses the typical sonata movements of these three works, that is the first movements of the quintet, the suite and the third quartet, one discovers an increasing refinement and intellectual emphasis upon technical aspects of the development section. The principle of continual variation slowly pervades all aspects of the structure; it becomes more and more the true kernel of sonata form. In this we can see Schoenberg's relationship to the technique of Brahms.

The third quartet was composed at the request of Elizabeth Sprague Coolidge, the generous American benefactor of modern music, to whom Schoenberg also dedicated it. It was performed for the first time on 19 September 1927 in Vienna by the Kolisch Quartet at a concert arranged by Mrs Coolidge. Schoenberg had spent his fifty-third birthday with his Viennese friends. The new style of the work led to penetrating discussions about the twelve-note technique. Schoenberg used it here with certain liberties which are absent from the first twelve-note works, such as repetitions of notes in the first movement, where the five notes G–E–D sharp–A–C form an *ostinato* which is kept up for twelve bars. But more important than the technical licences, which Schoenberg acknowledged, was the splendidly musical character of the work. When one heard the perfect interpretation given by the Kolisch Quartet (who played it, like all their repertoire, from memory) one almost forgot the demands which its four-part writing made on the ear.

After his great success in Vienna Schoenberg returned to Berlin in the autumn full of confidence. It seemed as if modern music was about to gain increasing influence there. Paul Hindemith, one of the most gifted of the younger German

composers, had come from Frankfurt as a teacher in composition to the Hochschule fuer Musik. Under the leadership of
Otto Klemperer the second State Opera—the Krolloper—was
opened at the newly rebuilt house on the Platz der Republik
—this institution, both in its repertoire and in the performances
of the works, was particularly receptive to experiments.
Klemperer already felt close to Schoenberg in their mutual
passionate admiration for Mahler. Alexander von Zemlinsky,
who belonged to Schoenberg's closest circle, later became
Klemperer's assistant. Nevertheless it took three years before
the long-overdue Berlin performance of Schoenberg's two
one-act operas took place; these had been given for the first
time, one in Prague and the other in Vienna. The Berlin
première was in July 1930, thus at the end of the season.
Erwartung was conducted by Zemlinsky, *Glueckliche Hand* by
Klemperer; already an increasing nationalistic movement was
beginning which was soon to demand and receive the Krolloper
as a sacrifice.

During the academic year of 1927-28 Schoenberg worked
on a score in which he used the experience he had gained in the
new technique in chamber music for the larger structure of the
orchestra. In September 1928 he completed it in Roquebrune
on the French Riviera. This was the Orchestral Variations
opus 31, which Wilhelm Furtwangler played for the first time
on December 2 of the same year in the Berlin Philharmonie
to an unreceptive public. The work, a significant study in the
expanded technique of variation allowed by the twelve-note
method, also widened the limits of orchestral polyphony. It is a
score of the boldest mastery, from the impressionistic sounds of
its introduction to the use of the B-A-C-H motif and the
astonishing coda which sums up all the possibilities explored
in the work. Schoenberg's personal style appears here in a
purer and even more unmistakable manner than in any of

his previous works since the development of the twelve-note technique.

Besides the instrumentation of Bach's E flat major organ prelude and fugue, 1928 also brought the beginning of a dramatic work—the first since *Glueckliche Hand*, which had been completed in 1913. Characteristically this time it is a comedy, a social satire without any higher literary ambitions, whose author hides behind the pseudonym of Max Blonda. By taking four people or two couples (with the addition of a child with a small speaking part) the inconstancy of modern man in things of love and art is demonstrated. The husband, a little tired of his wife, is attracted to her woman friend. The wife overcomes this marital crisis by using mondaine allurements. The two friends, male and female, pay a surprise visit on them and find them as a couple who have decided on a happy married life. With some regretful remarks about such old-fashioned views, the friends depart. 'Mama, what are they, modern people?' the child asks finally, after the father has stated that such views change from one day to the next. *Von heute auf morgen* ('From one day to the next') is the title of the opera, a one-acter which was completed on 3 August 1929 and was given the opus number 32.

This score, which uses the twelve-note method in a masterly fashion, is written for double to treble wind, normal strings, two saxophones, many kinds of percussion instruments, flexatone, piano, celesta, mandoline and guitar. Within the framework of the method Schoenberg achieves an astonishing amount of freedom in melody, counterpoint and form. What is particularly striking in this work is the great wealth of contrapuntal invention; this is, moreover, almost the servant of the drama in a Mozartian way. The canonic forms in which, for example, the quarrel duet between man and wife, as well as the quartet towards the end of the work, are cast are of a complexity for which there is no parallel in modern operatic music.

Particularly distinctive, however, is the treatment of the voices. They go far beyond the George songs in the boldness of their intervals and beyond the Petrarch Sonnet of the *Serenade* in rhythmical subtlety. And yet they are grateful to sing—in a way quite new for Schoenberg. Apart from the strictly written contrapuntal ensembles, the score contains a mass of highly vocal arioso ideas. The instrumentation, in spite of the independence of its part-writing, is yet so restrained that the vocal parts remain audible.

The difficulties of the work in performance are considerable, on account of its complicated structure; but the singers at the first performance found their work considerably easier after they had got to know the construction of the work as based on the row. For the whole work is again built on the twelve-note row: D-E flat-A-C sharp-B-F-A flat-G-E-C-B flat-F sharp, and on its three other forms. The first performance, which took place at the Frankfurt Opera in January 1930, had been prepared for many months by Hans W. Steinberg.[1] Musically and scenically (the producer was Dr Herbert Graf) it was excellent, coinciding in all essential points with the strange style of the work—a mixture of the fashionable and the esoteric. Shortly afterwards, Schoenberg himself conducted a broadcast performance of the opera in Berlin. Since then the work was not heard again for many years.

Von heute auf morgen was in many respects a child of sorrow for its creator. Schoenberg believed, probably impressed by attempts like Ernst Krenek's *Jonny spielt auf* or Hindemith's *Neues vom Tage*, that a light opera with a modern plot would bring him a wider public success. The Berlin publishing house,

---

[1] Now Dr William Steinberg, well known as a conductor in America and England.

Bote and Bock, which was to have printed the score and distributed it, was prepared to make unusual financial concessions. But Schoenberg demanded more than the firm was prepared to risk, quarrelled with the publisher, and published the very expensive piano score himself. This meant a considerable financial sacrifice for him, though it was mostly retrieved by the first performance.

The fact that the opera was not a sensational success and only received a moderate number of performances was due above all to the difficulty of its musical language, which, in spite of the lightness of its subject and its setting, did not easily win over an average public. To this it must be added that Germany at this time was already exposed to reactionary currents in its cultural life, which preceded the anti-modernistic retrograde aesthetic of the National Socialist mass taste. Modern operatic experiments, whether by Stravinsky, Kurt Weill, Milhaud George Antheil, or by Schoenberg himself, were being already fought by an organised opposition. Already the public as well as the newspapers were subconsciously taking a stand against everything that deviated from the taste of the petty bourgeois. A false sociological conception of the arts, which was already widespread in the early twenties in Germany, and during the Hitler years wanted to tie everything to the Procrustean bed of popular appreciation, viewed modern music as a dangerous symptom of the time as much as expressionist painting or surrealist poetry. This conception also affected a part of the intelligentsia, who believed that modern man could be saved by the music of amateurs and folklore. How little Schoenberg tended to give in to such ideas is proved by every bar, every word he produced. The critical years in America proved that he was a genius in lack of compromise and absolute intransigence as far as artistic matters were concerned. If he appeared to give in to fashionable tendencies of the time, as in the light opera, he did this only in order to criticise them more effectively and ironically.

In the course of the last Berlin years, from 1930 to 1933, Schoenberg and his family did a good deal of travelling. At the same time as Franz Schreker, he discovered for himself the beauty of the South. Schreker moved to a house in Estoril, not far from Lisbon. The Schoenberg family, who had lived for some time on the French Riviera, in 1931 found a house near Barcelona where they spent several months. The place, surrounded by hills, was called Bachada de Briz, and when Schoenberg later moved into his house in California, he was often reminded of his Spanish sojourn with its view of Barcelona by the great similarity of the view of Los Angeles which he had there.

1930 saw the composition of *Begleitungsmusik zu einer Lichtspielszene* (Accompaniment music to a Film Scene) opus 34 (later published by Heinrichshofen in Magdeburg), and the Six Pieces for male choir opus 35. The film music, in three episodes, attempts by unusual musical means to illustrate situations of great spiritual tension: imminent danger, fear and catastrophe. This is descriptive music in the strict sense, written with a light hand but which nevertheless deeply moves the sub-conscious as only music can do. Klemperer performed the work that year for the first time at the Berlin Krolloper. Three years later Nicolas Slonimsky conducted it in the giant auditorium of the Hollywood Bowl, little knowing that the composer would soon be living permanently only a few miles from this open-air starlit concert hall.

The choral pieces again present Schoenberg as his own librettist. They are written for unaccompanied male voices, and up to a point are technically linked to the choral pieces opus 27 and 28, though they are simpler in style. The last of the pieces, *Verbundenheit*, employs triads in a manner that is unusual in the later Schoenberg, and ends with a D minor 6/4 chord.

In the course of these years there also matured a plan for a composition of vastly greater dimensions and exceptional spiritual breadth. It was begun in 1930 in Berlin and Lugano, and was two-thirds completed in Barcelona in 1932. This is the three-act opera *Moses und Aron*. This work, which again has a libretto by Schoenberg himself, deals with the most difficult problems of philosophy and art. Conceived for a gigantic ensemble of soloists, choruses, orchestral players, ballet dancers and unusual scenic requirements, the work goes far beyond the limits of a normal operatic production.

While Schoenberg was working on the second act of *Moses und Aron* his wife Gertrud bore him the first child of his second marriage, a daughter, born on 7 May 1932, who was christened Nuria.[1] Shortly after the birth the little family returned to Berlin where Schoenberg, after a long break, resumed his courses. In his flat at the Nuernberger Platz his pupils and a few extraneous visitors met together for instruction in musical analysis, in which Schoenberg's knowledge and the wealth of his imagination became apparent to all.

This apartment, in a central quarter of the new West Berlin, was Schoenberg's last permanent residence in Europe, and it completely corresponded to the taste of its owner. His desk had been designed by Schoenberg himself, and he also himself made a small stepladder, worked in a spiral around a vertical axis. Among the furnishings of the music room were a piano and a harmonium, also a guitar and a mandoline, instruments which were frequently used for trying out sound effects. One large room was almost exclusively furnished with a ping-pong table; here Schoenberg played table tennis with his wife and friends—a game in which he excelled. He demonstrated a lively interest in new inventions, new materials and similar matters.

[1] Now the wife of the Italian composer Luigi Nono.

For his dining table he preferred chromium to silver because of its characteristic colour.

Chess too was often played in Schoenberg's home. But it was typical of him that he found the conventional game with its sixty-four squares and thirty-two pieces insufficient. He invented an enlarged game which he called 'Hundred-chess' with ten times ten squares. To the usual chessmen he added a bishop and an admiral; the number of pawns was increased to ten.

Yet despite the calm which characterised his way of life and his work in these years, Schoenberg remained conscious of the increasing and threatening political tension in Germany. He sympathised with the propagandists neither of the right nor the left. As a means of combating political confusion and social misery he recommended an administration led by the best professional people and vastly increased salaries for the workers. He did not himself wish to deal in politics and doubted if intellectuals without any special political education had anything useful to contribute.

The final work which Schoenberg completed in Germany was a new version of a cembalo concerto by Georg Matthias Monn (1717-1750) which he arranged for cello and orchestra. So closed the circle which had begun in 1912 with Schoenberg's edition of works of Austrian baroque music for the *Denkmaeler der Tonkunst in Oesterreich*. Here also it had been to G. M. Monn from Lower Austria, as well as to Johann Christian Mann, that Schoenberg had turned in his editorial work.

1933 marked the advent of Hitler and his party to power. Even if Schoenberg had not been of Jewish descent, and thus in the eyes of the National Socialists a second-class human being, they would never have forgiven him for his music. The prophets of the new Teutonic culture had for some time stigmatised this music in their manifestos as degenerate and 'foreign'. Now Schoenberg's teaching activities were attacked in a lying manner. One could read in the Nazi press that the master was inciting his pupils to despise all tradition and to hate all classical and romantic music.

For some months Schoenberg remained quietly in Berlin; he decided only in May, after receiving pressing advice from his friends abroad, to leave Germany. On 30 May 1933 he and Franz Schreker were dismissed from their positions—which, according to their contracts, were permanent!—by the Prussian Ministry of Culture. A cultural darkness descended over Germany which according to its originator was to last a thousand years. It lasted for a period of twelve years, but ended with an apocalyptic disaster which almost brought about the total destruction of Western culture. Schoenberg fled from the apocalyptic horsemen. Together with some of the best of Western artists and scientists, he carried the European cultural ideas for which he was responsible to a secure place.

NEW WORLDS

FRANCE first became Schoenberg's home. He could have chosen Austria or Czechoslovakia, but he was more attracted by the climate and style of life of western Europe. After a short stay in Paris, the family spent the summer in Arcachon, not far from Bordeaux. After eight years of living in complete material ease, Schoenberg now suddenly found himself without means. His income from the Prussian State was blocked; there were no longer royalties from Germany and his publishers could help only in a small way. Thus Schoenberg was forced to seek a teaching post. In Paris, where he returned in the autumn of 1933, he could not find one. But he received an offer from Boston; the Malkin Conservatory, a relatively small teaching institution (for example it had no orchestra), offered him the chair of composition. After brief reflection he accepted.

Before leaving France, however, Schoenberg took a step which was characteristic of him. Though he was of Jewish blood, he had been a Catholic in his childhood, and since the age of eighteen a Protestant. As soon as he had left Germany Schoenberg decided to become Jewish again. So on 24 July 1933, in a special ceremony in Paris, he was received back into the religion of his fathers. He became part of a community which was to undergo one of its most severe trials under the Nazi terror.

During these early months of emigration he wrote a work which was linked to the tradition of arranging works of older musicians—J. S. Bach, J. C. Mann and G. M. Monn. Schoenberg arranged a concerto grosso by Handel (no. 7 from opus 6) for string quartet and orchestra. He thought of it as a piece for the repertory of the Kolisch Quartet, with whom he was friendly; they gave the work its first performance and played it repeatedly.

The French boat which took Schoenberg to the United States arrived in New York on 31 October. A legendary reputation as a teacher had preceded him; demands by pupils to enter his classes at the Malkin Conservatory grew; fees for private lessons rose steeply. But the work that Schoenberg had accepted was greater than he anticipated, for the Malkin Conservatory held classes in both Boston and New York. Thus Schoenberg taught in both places, which meant frequent travelling between the two towns. Added to the strain were the sharp temperature fluctuations of the New York climate. In a short time the results became apparent; Schoenberg fell so seriously ill in January 1934 that the doctor in attendance gave him only a fortnight to live. The two concerts for which the Boston Symphony Orchestra had engaged him as guest conductor on 12 and 13 January had to be cancelled.

However, by March his health had already improved sufficiently for a substitute concert to take place in Boston. On March 16 Schoenberg conducted there the first performance in America of his *Pelleas und Melisande*. But he heeded the warning signs and decided to leave New York. The summer was spent in Chautuaqua in New York State—an elegant resort with something of a musical tradition. Besides regular orchestral concerts, courses took place there, but Schoenberg did not take part in these.

For reasons of health Schoenberg moved to Los Angeles in the autumn of 1934. The Californian climate with its dry heat, cool evenings and nights, and its happy mixture of sea and mountain air, had already attracted numerous other European artists and intellectuals. It also proved itself beneficial to Schoenberg. At first he was received as eagerly as in New York and Boston. Magic instructional cures were expected from him, and many of the younger and older film composers came to him to learn 'his tricks', as Oscar Levant put it in his much-read book, *A Smattering of Ignorance*. They were then greatly disappointed when he demanded that they should harmonise chorales or write clean four-part exercises. But, besides many who left him after a few weeks, there were also some who studied composition seriously with him, among them Dika Newlin, Gerald Strang and Leonard Stein.

It was only to be expected that the film producers should come to notice the great European musician who had now established himself in Hollywood. Schoenberg's *Accompaniment Music to a Film Scene* had been performed by Nicolas Slonimsky in the Hollywood Bowl. In 1935 Metro-Goldwyn-Mayer was preparing a film based on Pearl S. Buck's *The Good Earth*. The producer, Irving Thalberg, planned to use Schoenberg as its composer. To the question what would be his conditions for this task Schoenberg replied (as Hans W. Heinsheimer tells us in his book *Menagerie in F sharp*): 'Fifty thousand dollars and an absolute guarantee that nothing will be changed in my score.' With these words his relations with the film industry were clarified once and for all: i.e. broken off.

The first largish work which Schoenberg wrote in America was intended for a practical purpose—for the repertory of the American school orchestras, which were steadily increasing in numbers and in importance. Here regard had to be paid to the ease with which the piece could be played and understood. It was a case, so to speak, of a piece of Gebrauchsmusik (music for use), a solution of a not just purely artistic problem, but of a mainly educational one. This is the reason for the

Richard Fish

Schoenberg's work room in Los Angeles

A photograph taken toward the end of Schoenberg's life

simple tonal language of the String Suite in G, which was written in 1934 and was the first of several of Schoenberg's works to be published by G. Schirmer of New York (previously only a brief piano piece, opus 33b, had been published by an American firm). This work, though, goes technically far beyond its original purpose.

The return to tonality, as shown in the string suite, has been much misinterpreted. Some believed that Schoenberg was capitulating before the practical realism of America and thus with his new score was repudiating his previous works. Yet his next works—the violin concerto and the fourth string quartet—already refuted this idea. However, later it was pressed even more emphatically when Schoenberg published three further tonal compositions.

There can, though, be no question of a 'turning-back'. It meant no turning back when Mozart wrote in *Don Giovanni* an aria for Elvira in Handel's style, or when Max Reger wrote his suite 'in the old style'. An advance to new forms does not prevent one occasionally expressing oneself in the old ones; nothing is repudiated thereby. In fact in the arts nothing can be repudiated. Certain phenomena, such as the overcoming of tonality and functional harmony or the emancipation of the dissonance, cannot be revoked, and a thought once expressed continues to point a way. Even Richard Strauss did not go back on the new harmony and sound effects of *Salome* and *Elektra* when he preferred a simpler language in *Rosenkavalier*.

Schoenberg himself spoke about these assertions, with their malicious undertone regarding the 'Mistake of Atonality'. In an essay *On revient toujours* (*Stimmen*, Monatsblaetter fuer Musik, no. 16, September 1949, later reprinted in *Style and Idea*) he writes: 'It was not given to me to continue writing in the style of *Verklaerte Nacht* or the *Gurrelieder* or even of *Pelleas und Melisande*. Fate led me along a harder road. But the wish

H

remained constantly within me to return to the earlier style, and from time to time I give in to this desire.'

However unsuited Schoenberg proved himself to serve the musical conceptions of the film industry, just because of his artistic intransigence his reputation as a teacher and theoretician grew all the more. In California there were no musical conservatories with the older traditions of the Chicago Musical College, or of the standing of the Juilliard School, the Curtis Institute or the Eastman School of Music. But two important universities in Los Angeles had developed a certain rivalry, even in artistic matters. In contrast to European universities, where usually only musicology is taught (i.e. history, theory, acoustics and perhaps the sociology of music), the American universities often have complete music schools. It is possible to take all instrumental subjects, singing, theory and composition at the musical colleges of the universities up to degree level. The best American and foreign teachers are engaged for this purpose. Of the two universities of Los Angeles, the University of Southern California (U.S.C.) was the first to approach Schoenberg as early as 1935, and he accepted a professorship in composition there. Yet already in 1936 he left this position to take up a similar one with the University of California at Los Angeles (U.C.L.A.).

Schoenberg celebrated his sixtieth birthday in 1934 in California. As on his fiftieth birthday, the Viennese journal *Anbruch* (Universal Edition) again published a special number. It contained contributions by a friend of his youth, D. J. Bach, by his pupil and friend, Alban Berg, and by Paul A. Pisk, Erwin Stein, Anton Webern, Egon Wellesz and the critic Paul Stefan; these had already congratulated him in 1924. In addition there were such new names as Hans Erich Apostel (a gifted composer of the Schoenberg and Alban Berg school), Alois Hába (the Czech composer and exponent of the quarter-tone system), Alma Maria Mahler, Darius Milhaud, Olga Novakovic, the biographer of Alban Berg Willi Reich, and Alexander Zemlinsky. Some of them were soon to follow Schoenberg to America; Pisk, Stefan, Alma Mahler, Milhaud and Zemlinsky found asylum in the United States after Austria had become Fascist.

The age limit for professors at American universities was sixty-five. For Schoenberg it was, exceptionally, raised by five years, so that he could continue his academic teaching until 1944. Teaching at an American State University meant a change from his former practice of instruction. Many of his pupils had to be taught elementary questions of theory, and only a minority had either the wish or the gift to become composers. Thus Schoenberg developed here something which he called 'Ear-training through composition'—a schooling of the ear achieved through practical exercises in composition.

1936, the year in which Schoenberg joined the teaching faculty of the University of California, also produced, as the most important work of his first American creative period, the concerto for violin and orchestra opus 36 (completed on 23 September). Jokingly, Schoenberg said of this work that it needed a violinist with six fingers. This three-movement piece is in fact of breathtaking difficulty. Yet once the technical problems are mastered the soloist can attain an outstanding virtuosity. Despite its uncompromising musical character, it is a grateful piece of striking, almost daemonic effect. In contrast to the string suite, it is purely dodecaphonic, being built on a twelve-note row. Its shape corresponds to classical forms: a fast movement (Poco allegro) is succeeded by a slower one (Andante grazioso), and a lively march forms the finale. The synthesis of three elements gives the work a special, quite particular, character—strict development from the rules of twelve-note technique, soloistic autonomy of the violin part, and totally new sound ideas derived from a virtuosic accumulation of enormous intervals, harmonics in double-stopping and a simultaneous exploitation of unusual registers.

At this time, when this highly difficult work was being written—a work which, in spite of all its violinistic magic, is strictly based on the loftiest traditions—one of the strangest musical friendships was born. In Hollywood Schoenberg met George Gershwin, the much younger but famous composer of the *Rhapsody in Blue* and the negro opera *Porgy and Bess*. These two very different characters met in their mutual passion for tennis, and soon became very fond of each other. Gershwin certainly did not understand much of Schoenberg's music, even though he showed a strong sympathetic interest in it and also in Alban Berg's *Wozzeck*, and his own music (as is shown by parts of *Porgy and Bess*) was stimulated by the harmony of the Schoenbergian school. Levant reports (in *A Smattering of Ignorance*) that Gershwin said that he wanted to write something quite simple, a string quartet in the manner of Mozart, to which Schoenberg, a little annoyed, replied that Mozart was not at all simple. Gershwin was one of the first to whom Schoenberg announced, in the morning over a game of tennis, that his wife had given him a son. This was Rudolf Roland, born on 26 May 1937. Schoenberg was sixty-two and was to have a second son four years later—Adam Lawrence, born on 27 January 1941.

How close Gershwin was to Schoenberg can be understood by those who read the appreciation the older man broadcast about the younger. Gershwin died, aged thirty-eight, on 11 July 1937, in Los Angeles from the results of an operation for a brain tumour. In his appreciation Schoenberg calls him a great musician. And in an essay which he contributed in 1938 to Merle Armitage's book about Gershwin he explained this further. 'Many musicians', he writes, 'do not regard Gershwin a serious composer—that is, a man who lives in music and expresses everything, serious or not, sound or superficial, by means of music because music is his native language. There are a number of composers, serious ones (as they believe) or not (as I know), who have learned to add notes together. But they are only serious on account of a perfect lack of humour and soul.'

'It seems to me that this difference alone is sufficient to justify calling the one a composer, but the other none. An artist is to me like an apple tree: When his time comes, whether he wants it or not, he bursts into bloom and starts to produce apples. And as an apple tree neither knows nor asks about the value experts of the market will attribute to its product, so a real composer does not ask whether his products will please the experts of serious arts. He only feels he has to say something; and says it.

It seems to me beyond doubt that Gershwin was an innovator. What he has done with rhythm, harmony and melody is not merely style. It is fundamentally different from the mannerism of many a serious composer.'[1]

Gershwin was also a gifted painter, and in 1937—in one of his last pictures—he did an oil portrait of Schoenberg in which his mouth and eye, which were so characteristic of him, are reproduced with an astonishing likeness.

At about the same time as the violin concerto the fourth string quartet was written in Los Angeles; though it bears a higher opus number (opus 37) it was completed earlier, on 26 July 1936. In fact Schoenberg worked during this period on both works, and the first drafts of the violin concerto (which was only completed on 23 September) precede those of the quartet.

[1] From *George Gershwin*, edited and designed by Merle Armitage, Longmans, Green & Co, Ltd., 39 Paternoster Row, London, E.C.4, 1938.

Opus 37 is dedicated: 'To the ideal patron of chamber music, Elizabeth Sprague Coolidge, and the ideal interpreters, the Kolisch Quartet.' Ten years before, Schoenberg had already written his third quartet for Elizabeth Sprague Coolidge. This generous benefactress, who originated the Foundation in the Library of Congress which bears her name, had since 1925 commissioned compositions from many leading modern composers, such as Béla Bartok, Alfredo Casella, G. Francesco Malipiero, Walter Piston, Sergei Prokofiev and Igor Stravinsky.

The fourth quartet, like the second and the third, is in four movements; in the first quartet the underlying division into four movements is fused by connecting passages. As in the third quartet, the technique of composition with twelve notes is dominant. The four movements (Allegro molto; Commodo; Largo; Allegro) are based on a single row. It appears in the normal mirror forms, and also transposed and in various subdivisions, which are most skilfully related to one another. The style, compared with that of 1927, is free and masterly throughout. In comparing the works of the two periods, one gains the impression that in the third quartet the method still controlled the invention, while here, within a kaleidoscopic world of variations related to one another, absolute freedom of choice reigns. The wealth of variety of forms that are possible within the method is so great that, in practice, the imagination is hedged around by no limitations. With this regained freedom the musical language is reanimated in such a way that romantic feeling on a higher plane often seems to be restored to it. The magnificent Largo of the fourth quartet, an arioso scena which begins with the four instruments playing a dramatic recitative in unison, and sustains its homophonic character, even when accompanying figures strive for greater independence, is contemplative music of the highest

order. The form of this movement is clearly binary, and the repetition of the introductory unison in inversion has the effect of a new perspective within the same musical panorama.

In the first and last movements one can easily recognise the types of sonata movement and rondo, and in the second movement the Beethoven type of scherzo. But the forms here are not abstract, as for example in the wind quintet, but filled with a new significance. Besides its twelve-note character, which Leibowitz so convincingly demonstrates, the quartet is constructed within the framework of the classical periodic forms, as Josef Rufer (in *Stimmen*, vol. 16, Berlin 1949) has shown from the same example, the main theme of the first movement.

The first performance of opus 37 took place in 1937 by the Kolisch Quartet in Los Angeles; it was followed by numerous performances in America.

In 1938 Schoenberg wrote a work which had been commissioned by a Jewish organisation—*Kol Nidre* for Rabbi, chorus and orchestra, opus 39—a composition of greatly extended tonality which uses the ancient Kol Nidre theme of the Jewish liturgy. How seriously Schoenberg regarded this commission is proved by the catalogue of his articles; for 1938 it mentions three different manuscripts—*Studies for Kol Nidre*, *About Kol Nidre* and *Notes on Kol Nidre and the Four-Point Programme*. This programme itself was written at this time.

Kol Nidre is Hebrew, meaning 'All Vows'. The repentant sinner is freed by prayer from promises which might bring him into opposition to God. But the evening prayer that precedes the Kol Nidre opens with a conjuration spoken by the Rabbi to the assembly. It contains a kind of Genesis, which is borrowed from the Kabbala. At the climax of the conjuration come the words *Bischiwo Schel Malo, Uwischiwo Schel Mato*, meaning in English, 'In the name of those above and in the name of those on earth'. Then follows by the permission of the community to pray together with the sinners. The whole ceremony takes place on the eve of Yom Kippur, the feast of reconciliation.

Schoenberg gave both parts, the conjuration and the actual Kol Nidre, a new and very personally inspired form in the English language. He dealt similarly with the liturgical melody. It has come to us from collections of the nineteenth century, when cantors such as Salomon Sulzer, Moritz Deutsch and Louis Lewandowski made arrangements of the Jewish songs. But their synagogue music, as Leonid Sabanieff has noted, is influenced by Catholic and Protestant musical cultures. Abraham Idelsohn, the greatest authority on Jewish music, finds in the various parts of the Kol Nidre melody Spanish elements from the sixteenth century and coloraturas from the eighteenth century, intermingled with ancient motifs like the Esther melody and the Prophetic songs. The beauty of the theme has also attracted non-Jewish composers; Max Bruch built on it his adagio on Hebraic melodies for cello, and Emil Reznicek in 1923 based the overture to his opera *Holofernes* on it.

In the main Schoenberg uses the first five bars of the melody, which are of Spanish origin and which can be found as No. 267 in Pedrell's catalogue of Catalan songs.

The intervals of the opening bars, falling minor second and

major third, become motivic elements and appear for the most part unaltered. The interval of a fifth in the third bar acquires motivic significance. In both cases Schoenberg keeps to the tonal, functional property of the intervals, and only the basic tonality is changed. Schoenberg's *Kol Nidre* is a tonal work; it is written in G minor and ends in G major. With it he continues the series which began with the G major suite for string orchestra, composed in 1934 in America, and to which the organ variations of 1943 and the G minor variations for wind orchestra of 1944 also belong. In his later works, i.e. after the development of the twelve-note technique, Schoenberg saw no appreciable difference between tonal and atonal music; in fact the structure of either group of works demonstrates the same compositional technique. It is the technique of permanent or continued variation. Typical of this is the way in which the melismatic motif of the penultimate bar in Schoenberg's introduction is chromatically varied, completely within the spirit of oriental music, and the way in which this chromatic variation itself is worked in the mirror forms of the old Netherlands school—which is comparable to the dodecaphonic methods of the fourth string quartet and the *Ode to Napoleon*, the twelve-note works written before and after *Kol Nidre*.

Kol Nidre is written for speaking voice, mixed chorus and small orchestra. It is in two parts which correspond to the liturgy. The first, fifty-seven bars long, of which half is orchestral introduction, accompanies the opening of the book of Sohar and the reading of the conjuration. The chord sequence G minor, E flat minor, B flat major, E flat minor, has the note B flat in common, held in the flute and horn, while at the same time the divided celli, muted, sul ponticello, tremolando, may be heard playing the notes G-F sharp-D-F sharp. The chromatic oriental melisma follows on from the held B flat. On the repetition of the chord sequence an important falling bass figure distinguishes itself; it is played by bass clarinet and celli pizzicato, and consists of the notes G, E flat, B flat, F sharp, a version of the E flat major triad in downwards arpeggio to which the F sharp is added as a minor third. This acquires motivic significance during the course of the piece.

Here the relationship of the *Kol Nidre* with the *Ode to Napoleon* becomes clear. The twelve-note row of the latter is so constructed that the tonalities of E flat minor, G minor and B minor continually alternate with one another.

With the words of the Rabbi 'The Kabbalah tells us' a new 6/8 movement opens pianissimo. After 'Let there be Light' there follows a sharp uprushing figure on three clarinets, a flexatone trill with a stroke on steel bells, a flash of lightning in high strings and woodwind. This very picturesque tone painting is achieved by strictly motivic means. With the Moderato that follows, the absolution from the vows begins, and with it the actual Kol Nidre. The first bars of the melody appear like a *canto fermo* in the woodwind. A real symphonic movement is built on the march-like rhythm. The chorus, in unison, sings the chief motif, now transposed to A flat minor. With the words 'We repent that these obligations have estranged us' the Prophetic melody appears. After an uncanny climax of colour introduced by the bass clarinet, and carried on by the oboes over a funeral-march-like *ostinato* in fifths on the basses, the chromatic melisma on the woodwind announces a very freely varied reprise, to the words of the Rabbi, 'Whatever binds us to falsehood.'

A cadence, which rapidly goes through the circle of the degrees of the scale and their related thirds, leads to the concluding G major triad. The score gives 22 September 1938 as the date when the work was completed. It is a day between Yom Kippur and the Feast of the Tabernacles.

This work, which is little known by the wider public, is

one of the best of Schoenberg's compositions; the art of its motivic variation is as great as its wealth of harmonic relations, which constantly move on the borders of tonality, yet without ever losing sight of it. For orchestral colour Schoenberg excelled it only in the opera *Moses und Aron*. It is an example of the manner in which the raw material of a folksong-like theme is employed for the highest purposes of variation and symphonic development—much more radically than, for example, the melody of *Aennchen von Tharau* in the suite opus 29 or *Lieber Augustin* in the F sharp minor quartet.

The three years that followed brought, in creative work, only the arrangement and completion of an earlier work, the second chamber symphony. This had been begun in 1906 at the same time as the first one, had been taken some way and then abandoned. In 1908 and 1911 Schoenberg took up the work again, and he completed it in 1940 as opus 38. It is again a tonal work, even if it is in the very free tonality that Schoenberg had developed in 1906. Simultaneously the techniques of the twelve-note method and the variants contained in the different mirror forms of the thematic material are radically employed here, so that the second movement of the work particularly is technically representative of the later Schoenberg. In the same year, 1940, Schoenberg became an American citizen.

In the meanwhile the Old World, with which Schoenberg felt himself most closely linked, presented a threatening aspect. The bloody adventures pursued by German Fascism seemed to seal the triumph of force. Austria, Schoenberg's mother country, had become as much a victim of German imperialism as Czechoslovakia, Poland or even France. The situation of the freedom-loving peoples of Europe, perhaps even of America, seemed hopeless; Hitler's pact with Japan and Italy meant immediate danger for the New World too. Then in 1942 the

United States entered the war, after Hitler himself, as a result of his attack on Russia, his ally of 1939, was facing war on two fronts.

The events of these years found a peculiar echo in Schoenberg's work, the *Ode to Napoleon*. In the diaries of Lord Byron there is found in the entry for 10 April 1814 (the day after Napoleon's resignation in Fontainebleau): 'Today I boxed for an hour, wrote an ode to Napoleon Bonaparte, made a fair copy of it, ate six rusks, drank four bottles of soda water, and browsed for the rest of the time'. The ode, written in sixteen verses of nine lines each, originally appeared anonymously. It was a passionate accusation, not only of the Corsican, but of every kind of dictatorship. It is not easy to find one's way through the welter of hints and similes which Byron heaps on top of one another to complete the picture of the inglorious general. Yet the power of poetic indignation is on a grand scale which makes these explosions into a work of art. A bizarre epilogue followed. Murray, Byron's publisher, wished to circumvent the law that demanded stamp duty on published material. He asked the poet for an addition, and Byron produced three further verses, ending with a homage to George Washington, the first President of the United States.

The nineteen verses remained forgotten for 127 years. Then Schoenberg discovered in Byron's ode thoughts of burning actuality. The pamphlet of 1814 became an anti-Fascist manifesto. Byron had anticipated Hitler; Schoenberg in composing the text anticipated his downfall. The composition, for speaking voice, string quartet and piano, was completed in 1942. It was given the opus number 41.

Schoenberg set this poem (including the three later verses that Byron eventually discarded) as a melodrama. With it he again took up a style that he had brilliantly employed in *Pierrot Lunaire* three decades earlier. Even though the score

contains all the peculiarities of the mature Schoenberg style
—the splitting up of the themes, the widely-spaced intervals,
the irregular rhythms—the music appeals more immediately
to the listener than many of his earlier works. It is filled with
an unusually ardent dramatic breath which carries along even
those whose unschooled ear might prevent the comprehension
of this work. Its ballad-like basic character wins through.
The *Ode*, performed for the first time by Arthur Rodzinski
with the baritone Mack Harrell in New York, is written
entirely within the twelve-note technique. The row which
Leibowitz deduces from bars 37-38 is so chosen that harmonically it provides triad-formations as material. Through its use

and, so to speak, cadential quality it often produces the impression of a firm tonality, and it is not by chance that this opus
closes with a kind of E flat major cadence. The whole piece,
compared with the twelve-note works of the twenties and
thirties, is infinitely more relaxed, and harsh sounds of a
cacophonous kind which are difficult to appreciate have been
eliminated. A certain impressionistic softness of the harmony
(as had occurred earlier in the opening bars of the Variations
opus 31) marks long passages, although whole cascades of
scorn and hatred are also poured on to the reviled dictator.

These characteristics are achieved by the employment of an
astonishing freedom in the treatment of the row. Its ingredients,
above all its three-note groups, are constantly mixed together,
and the use of only certain intervals and chords results in the
remarkably seamless quality of the texture which characterises
this work in particular. As typical of the predominating
cadences, one may quote the three final bars with their logical
tendency towards E flat.

To understand Schoenberg's spiritual and technical development, one should compare the *Ode to Napoleon* with the thirty-year-older *Pierrot Lunaire*. On the one hand the somewhat morbid mirroring of the self in a dandy-like verse-language of not unassailable dignity; on the other the confession of a flaming romantic song of hatred against tyranny. In *Pierrot* the flight from tonality and the emancipation of the dissonance are made legitimate through the return to old forms; the *Ode* shows a liberation from the orthodoxy of self-imposed law and order.

In the meantime the experience newly acquired from teaching in America found a creative outlet. A small book, *Models for Beginners in Composition*, shows in musical examples and in the method of instruction the most essential elements for composition teaching of an elementary kind. Schoenberg received the help of his pupil, the composer Gerald Strang, in putting the book together. He based it on a six weeks' composition course for students in California.

Yet another work was begun in 1942, and completed on the last day of the year, the concerto for piano and orchestra, opus 42. This work, in one movement but in four clearly distinguished sections (Andante; Molto allegro; Adagio; Giocoso), is strictly composed in the twelve-note technique and also forgoes the tonal effects that resulted from the choice of the row in the *Ode to Napoleon*. Only the last part, the Giocoso-Rondo, opens with a theme which circles around the note F sharp for twelve bars. In its unusual division of the balance between solo part and orchestra the piece—roughly twenty minutes long—continues the Brahms tradition. Even the virtuoso-like richness of the piano part stems from Brahms. The first ländler-like theme appears Viennese in its gentle gaiety, and the music returns to a gay character in the final rondo. But in the Molto Allegro we enter darker spheres, and the device of a four-part chord in harmonics on the piano (an effect which had already been used in 1909 in opus 11) leads us towards other worlds. They are the worlds of ghostlike sound which, in the Adagio, after a section for orchestra alone, lead to increasingly menacing and exciting figures; the music calms itself briefly in a kind of solo cadenza for the piano, and then disrupts the fabric with even greater violence into figural molecules. To pour out such drama and such lyrical moods, to explore the depths of psychology and anxiety in a completely articulated coherent form can only be successfully achieved by an imagination such as Schoenberg's. The piece, however it may be understood or misunderstood, is epoch-making; one cannot escape its effect. Whether the listener wants it or not, his spirit is affected by it.

Leopold Stokowski conducted the first performance in New York in the N.B.C. studio at the beginning of February 1944. Eduard Steuermann played the solo part, the same Steuermann who had belonged to the circle of Schoenberg's friends for more than thirty years and who had played many of his works for the first time.

The following year, too, brought two important compositions. They are the continuation of the line that had begun in 1934 with the string suite and had led via the *Kol Nidre* to the second chamber symphony. In them Schoenberg used the technical experiences of the twelve-note method in tonal composition. How fruitful these works proved themselves to be in the sense of a newly won freedom in composition could be demonstrated as much in the *Ode to Napoleon* with its triads and quasi-tonal cadences as in the masterly structure of the piano concerto. Now the reverse took place: a dialectical experience was completed. There was only one form which, within the framework of tonality, secured a similar variety out of the same basic idea, the variation form. From the start it had been Schoenberg's immanent form of musical thinking. In close symbiosis with the principle of development, it had led from Brahms through Reger to him; he had made it the dominating form of progressive compositional technique.

In 1941 Schoenberg wrote his first work for organ, Variations on a Recitative, opus 40. The work is in D minor, but a D minor which has lost its original nature through intense chromaticism. In his instrumental treatment of the organ Schoenberg demonstrates the same lack of prejudice with which he approached all artistic tasks. Unusual registration, tremoli, contrasting effects of the extreme registers, these things cast a most curious light on the piece. Two years later he wrote opus 43, Theme and Variations for Wind Orchestra; then he re-orchestrated this work for normal orchestra. The basic tonality, G minor, is clearly defined. Harmonically these seven variations on a broadly conceived theme of twenty-one bars are no more daring or extravagant than the works of the later Reger or Strauss's *Ariadne*. But what distinguishes it from almost all contemporary music is its unique synthesis of polyphony and harmonic thinking, the thematic and motivic relations of every line of its complicated structure. In the seven highly contrasted variations on the theme, among which an Adagio di Valse, a Fugato and the brilliant Finale are particularly impressive, there is a mastery of connection of thought and motivic division, an art of development, a variety of character, for which parallels can be only found among Schoenberg's own works. Compared with the Orchestral Variations opus 31 of fifteen years earlier, these are both richer and freer. The technical influence of Brahms is clear. Orchestrally, the principle of chamber-music-like writing is carried out with an amazing fullness of tone painting and a bold exploitation of the characteristic colours and registers of the instruments. The Organ Variations are closely related to those for orchestra in the technical sense; they have the effect of a lighter parallel work, if not a study for them.

In the summer of 1943 Carl Engel celebrated his sixtieth birthday in New York—he was one of the leading American musicologists and also chairman of the Gustav Schirmer publishing firm. (Engel's German grandfather had been the founder of the German Kroll Opera, where in 1930 Schoenberg's *Erwartung* and *Die glueckliche Hand* had been given). Schoenberg contributed a very ingenious occasional work to a special birthday issue published for the occasion by *The Musical Quarterly*. These are two three-part canons in D minor, strictly written in the Dorian mode. All the parts begin simultaneously but the second moves twice as fast as the first, the third twice as fast as the second. In the second canon events are further complicated by the use of three different clefs: at the end there is a modulation to D major. The text, by Schoenberg himself, ends with the words: 'Nonsense! that is silly trash! and only those who never have been young or have risked a foolish bluuder boast now of their wisdom. We who are of different stuff dare still to expose our faults, because we know; Life begins at sixty.'

Contrapuntal works of this kind were much to Schoenberg's liking. In his book *Style and Idea* he quotes the example of Brahms, citing the latter's words: 'If I don't feel like composing I write counterpoint'. But he states at the same time that good counterpoint needs inspiration just as much as all good music.

J

'Whether much or little effort is needed depends on circumstances which are outside our reach.' That surely is not the point of view of a pure constructivist and of one who subjects everything to the brain. Schoenberg, as far as his relations to the place of heart and brain in music are concerned, was nearer to Pfitzner's theory of inspiration than to the views of Stravinsky. Nevertheless, even within the sphere of the post-romantic tradition, with its over-emphasis on confused sentimentality, Schoenberg did more to clarify the issues radically than any other of his contemporaries. It is significant that he should have used a sentimental occasion, the sixtieth birthday of a friend, to draw on a form of a highly intellectual kind derived from the old Netherlands masters.

The following year provided an occasion for a celebration in Schoenberg's own home. His seventieth birthday fell in a time no less politically turbulent than his sixtieth. It was the late summer of 1944, and the overthrow of German Fascism, anticipated in the *Ode to Napoleon*, was imminent. As a result of the concentration of all of its strength into the war effort, America itself was in a highly critical and feverish period. Artistic events were pushed more and more into the background. Nevertheless Schoenberg received considerable homage from musicians of every sort. Among his own former pupils, Dr Heinrich Jalowetz wrote an essay in *The Musical Quarterly*, in which Darius Milhaud also published some reminiscences of Schoenberg. The excellent quarterly, *Modern Music*, published by Minna Ledermann, contained highly interesting contributions from Lou Harrison, Ernst Krenek and Kurt List, and the English periodical *Tempo* one from Roger Sessions.

Yet the completion of his seventh decade also brought difficulties. Schoenberg's teaching activities at the University of Los Angeles had already been extended beyond the usual age limit of sixty-five, and now had to cease. Schoenberg was given a pension, but since his pension was so low, in view of the short duration of his professorship of eight years, he had to begin to earn a living anew. Schoenberg bought a house with a large garden in a beautiful position lying on a hill in Brentwood Park on the western outskirts of Los Angeles. Here, in the large music room and studio, which contained a grand piano and also a harmonium, he taught his pupils—a cosmopolitan crowd of Europeans, Americans, and New Zealanders. His work with them (there were sometimes as many as fifteen) used up much of his time. This is the reason why he composed little in 1944 and 1945.

His next work was due to the popular song industry. A popular light American musician, Nat Shilkret, commissioned several serious musicians in Los Angeles to write a symphonic work on the Book of Genesis—the individual composers were to choose their own section of the book. Besides Schoenberg such different musicians as Mario Castelnuovo-Tedesco, Darius Milhaud, Stravinsky, Alexander Tansmann, Ernst Toch and Shilkret himself took part in this. Schoenberg chose as his theme the prologue to the Creation. The piece, which is called *Prelude*, has the opus number 44. It is a highly polyphonic, brief orchestral work with chorus.

In 1946 Schoenberg became seriously ill. Week by week he grew more feeble until one day his heart ceased to beat. Medically Schoenberg was dead. But the most unlikely thing happened: a doctor gave an injection into his heart, which began beating once more. 'I have risen from real death and now feel very well', Schoenberg wrote in a letter to the author of this book. Nevertheless certain incurable weaknesses remained from this illness. Schoenberg's eyesight was weakened to the point where he could no longer write on ordinary music paper. He used one that had been specially printed for him with lines that were about four times further apart than usual.

In 1946 the string trio opus 45 was written. This short piece in one movement had its première in 1947 on the occasion of a symposium of American music critics. It is one of the most interesting and imaginative works Schoenberg ever wrote. The use made of unusual registers and ways of playing the instruments, the dissonant, strict twelve-note technique, and the rapidly changing character of the music make it difficult of approach both for the performers and the listener.

There are three phenomena in modern artistic culture which have had an effect as profound but as confined in extent as, perhaps, Einstein's General Theory of Relativity has had in the scientific sphere. They are the inner monologues of James Joyce, the 'disassociation' of plastic art, with abstract painting as its final result, and the style of Arnold Schoenberg. Their limited sphere of influence is evident; this even provides opponents with their most important argument, which is daily repeated with gusto—that they find no response amongst the public and therefore are superfluous, unhealthy and damaging. On the other hand their effects in depth are rarely and reluctantly discussed. People do not want to acknowledge that without the constant encounter with elements of these modern arts our whole aesthetic existence would be as unthinkable as is modern science without Einstein's corrective theories. This fact is indisputable, and it may be just this which so excites the supporters of the pleasure-loving aesthetic. For no creative production that can be taken seriously is imaginable now, whether in the fields of poetry, painting, sculpture or music, without the influence of the inner monologue, disassociation or the Schoenberg style. Even in the mass productions of commercial art, in literature down to the wireless play and film dialogue, in painting down to the poster and industrial art, and in music down to compositions for films this 'effect in depth' is evident. It would be possible to say simply: those producing art-objects can no longer escape from these factors even if they should wish to do so, and even if they want to oppose them on aesthetic grounds. The public accepts them only through the roundabout way of the commercial arts.

A common tendency lies behind the novelties and enrichments of language as well as behind the theory of relativity; it could be called a revision of reality. Research into the origins of this tendency has been undertaken by analysts of different disciplines with not altogether satisfactory results, yet with certain outstanding individual successes: among these analysts are sociologists and psychologists, historians and philosophers, natural scientists and metaphysicians.

Schoenberg's music changed and developed technically in the course of his creative activity. Stylistically, already by 1906 it presented such a definite unity that almost no important new characteristic was added to it later. In this even the introduction of such a dominating structural technique as composition with twelve notes, with its aim of complete control, could alter nothing. Yet it is just this technique which has been made the subject of all analyses of his music for many years.

On the other hand the question of style, despite its vastly greater importance, has been neglected. 'Le style est l'homme' —the axiom must be understood in the way that the particular handwriting of a man is expressed in any of his activities, whether he writes, paints or makes music. Schoenberg did all three, and the works that resulted are of a personal and unmistakable kind. About his literary style, one of his first analysts, Dr Heinrich Jalowetz, said in 1911 that it showed the strictest regard for objectivity, contained no decorative adjectives but only substantive words, that the balance would be disturbed if even one sentence was deleted, and that the style sprang from the point of view, and the richness of language from the almost indescribable wealth of ideas. Paul Amadeus Pisk defined Schoenberg's musical style in 1924 as one in which truth took the place of beauty, and he mentioned as characteristics: big intervallic leaps, pauses used as part of the structure, and the abandonment of symmetry, sequences and repetitions. In a conversation Schoenberg himself once formulated it thus: 'Only what has not been said is worth saying'. This perhaps is the shortest formula for a whole complex of things which attract our attention in his music, and which also includes the avoidance of repetitions. Freud denounced the compulsion to repeat things as a neurotic symptom; the modern *ostinato* music has its roots in this compulsion as much as in the models of exotic percussion music. What, however, is this prohibition of repetition, this taboo that Schoenberg, for example, imposes on an exact reprise? We must interpret it as an urge towards Becoming, which will not be satisfied with Being felt as a state of poverty.

Now everything that we have heard in the way of definition of Schoenberg's musical language is rather fragmentary. Let us register more extensively and methodically the impressions of any chosen work after the liquidation of tonality, i.e. after 1908. It is possible to advance negatively and to note these characteristics: dissociation, i.e. juxtaposition of unconnected sections; breaking up of the syntax; arbitrary linking of ideas; alogicality of the harmony (if functional harmony be regarded as a criterion); asymmetry in the forms and their components; atonality, i.e. the lack of a pull towards a tonal centre; ametricality, i.e. the lack of a regular beat.

Or else the same signs can be evalued positively, and one can perhaps say: quick reaction, overflowing imagination, a wealth of thought, permanent variation, heightened sensitivity in the harmony; heightened expressive tension in the melody; increased possibilities of surprise in rhythm and periodicity, as

well as in the formal aspects; renunciation of traditional logic
to the point of psychic automatism.

Intervals increased to giant size can already be noted in the
melodic style of Schoenberg's early works, as in Tove's highly
expressive love song from the *Gurrelieder*, 'Nun sag' ich Dir
zum erstenmal', with major seventh and minor eleventh
succeeding each other rapidly in the sung part. They remain
an essential ingredient of Schoenberg's language; they are
shunned as unsingable intervals, yet they present the essential
element of a widely ranging melodic style. But basically they
are also linked with the seemingly contrary tendency to use
the smallest intervals and to chromatic movement by step.
Here a structural point becomes clear: Schoenberg's way of
thinking sees no functional distinction between a note and its
transposition into a higher, lower or double octave. For
example, in his music the succession G–F sharp can appear
as a semitone, a major seventh, a minor ninth or as an interval
an octave larger than these without changing its constructive
meaning thereby.

Amongst the things which are most painfully missed in
Schoenberg's music are triads and also all the chords which
one had become used to regard as consonances. Further,
expressed in general terms, it avoids everything obvious, in the
aesthetic as well as in the acoustic sense of the overtones near
to the fundamental note. Finally the sequence, as a form of
introducing the motifs or melodic shapes, is often felt to be
lacking. But to forgo these forms of the obvious is no more
than a consequential continuation of the quite clear tendency
of development in the German and Austrian classical traditions.
Whoever looks at Mozart's arrangement of Handel's *Messiah*
will be astonished at the lack of consideration and piety with
which a ballast of sequences and superfluous repetitions have
been discarded until the shorter work corresponds to the more

modern and sensitive nerves of a later era. We can define the renunciation of the obvious and of the sequence as the result of the greater artistic sensitivity and intelligence which is also demanded by the listener. The modern nervous constitution of the inhabitants of capital cities quickly tires of mere charm, and the more developed an intellect has become the more its sensitivity is increased.

Essentially listeners to music become more specialised and thus more limited, a fact much and strongly lamented by the aestheticians of mere pleasure. To this plaint one can only reply: he who evalues art by the number of its consumers must remain with Franz Lehar. Higher forms of art are things for the élite, not for the masses. In the introduction of his book *Lyrik des expressionistischen Jahrzehnts*, Gottfried Benn replies to the accusation of dehumanisation: 'Who was really still concerned with humanity? Perhaps science, this monstrous science in which there was nothing but unobvious concepts, artificial abstract formulae, the whole being an utterly senselessly constructed world in the Goethean sense? Here country villas, observatories and Indian temples were devoted to theories which in the whole world were understood by only eight specialists, of whom five doubted them; but if a poet applied himself to a special word-experience, a painter to his special discovery in colour, this was regarded as anarchistic, formalist, even a mockery of the people.'

The trio is full of such creative experiences. It is so significant and clear an example of Schoenberg's personal style that one could base a comprehensive stylistic analysis on it. It was written in five short weeks in the late summer—from 20 August to 23 September 1946. Thomas Mann reported in his *Creation of Dr Faustus*: 'One must bear in mind here a meeting with Schoenberg at which he told me of his new, just completed trio, and of the experiences of his life that he secreted in the composition; this work in a certain sense is a precipitation of them. He declared that he described his illness and medical treatment including "male nurse" and the rest in it.'

The highly expressive language of the trio possibly reflects impressions from the no-man's-land between life and death. René Leibowitz, in his *Introduction à la musique de douze sons*, has made a technical analysis of it;[1] the row out of which Schoenberg constructs it is not twelve, but eighteen notes long, and the three six-note groups are in mirror relationships to one another. It is not, however, these technical procedures which are interesting but the formal idea that they serve. And one notices above all in the trio that it contains reprises, repetitions of small groups of bars. The work is in three parts or sections without breaks. The first two parts are again subdivided so that an episode follows each main section. The main section of the first part consists of fifty-one bars, the first episode of eighty-one bars; the main section of the second part, beginning as a slow waltz with falling sixths on the violin, corresponds somewhat in its forty-seven bars to the main section of the first part; but the second episode with its twenty-four bars is only a third as long as the first episode. The first episode begins, with almost Tristan-like romanticism, with a *dolce* phrase on the violin over a held third, A–C sharp, on the viola and cello. Then follows a short cantabile phrase in a low register that dissolves in ever more restless movement and is lost in a rising violin phrase which ends in the region of the high harmonics. A recitative section with a falling glissando is transposed up a semitone twenty-five bars later. The second episode is characterised by a closely worked canonic passage, and by the glissandi which follow, now played fortissimo and falling to a stubbornly repeated *feroce* figure. Also a passage in unison stands

[1] See however Schoenberg's remarks on this, quoted by Josef Rufer in his *Composition with Twelve Notes*, p. 106.

out from the otherwise very complex writing. The third part,
eighty-six bars long, begins with a note-for-note reprise of the
beginning, though only for one bar; already in the second bar
there are variations; the third bar is left out altogether, but the
fourth and fifth bars appear unaltered. Then two bars are left
out, the next two are repeated unaltered, then the next two
are omitted; then comes a literal reprise of the two following
ones. Then an idea in sevenths and ninths pizzicato on the
violin appears in a compressed version of that at the
beginning.

The whole formal structure of the first main part is here
shortened and compressed through simple telescoping or
through subtle syntheses of ideas. So the reprise of the Tristan-
esque romantic idea which begins the episode appears much
earlier than in the first part. This too is abbreviated by the
omission of two bars. We are thus dealing here with an
ingenious technique which is called the 'shortened reprise'.
And shortly before the closing development section we again
meet the recitative from the first episode, now in inversion,
with the glissando upwards and the plucked arpeggio that
follows downwards.

These clearly apparent repetitions allow the form of the
whole to become very visible. They take on here the sense of
point of contact, of relation back to the original, but without
becoming a mechanical repetition of what has already been
said; through its noticeable omissions this has the effect
of a built-up 'montage'. In connection with Schoenberg's later
music people have often spoken of athematicism, which he
himself by the way emphatically denied. Certainly this music
is not thematic in the sense of classical procedures. This is
forbidden by the special dialectic of the twelve-tone method.
But, in a technique which can be followed thematically and
motivically, it presents shapes which can often be grouped

differently in new and surprising combinations of known elements like figurations in a kaleidoscope.

This is also true of the harmony. It is derived from the row, and several times becomes independent in the otherwise highly contrapuntal fabric. This already happens after the middle of the first main section, when a number of six-part chords are drummed out nine times in semiquavers for four bars. Before this, however, these chords had been developed, so to speak, out of different combinations of three major sevenths, shuffled about one with the other, until all their sound-possibilities were exhausted. Every repetition here is so infinitely removed from the pleasing aspect of 'once upon a time', through abbreviation, variation, mirror inversion, permutation and transposition, and made so different from the form in which it first appeared that it is rather to be comprehended empirically as a surrealist measure of psychical automatism rather than as a move 'back to convention'. And in this lies the inner affinity between this style and the attempt at denaturalisation which Stravinsky has undertaken with the forms of classical music in his so-called neo-classical works.

As far as the style of the trio is concerned, it should be said that even for Schoenberg it contains a quite exorbitant accumulation of varying tone colours on the three strings—an alternations of harmonics, pizzicato, bowed and struck *col legno*, and heightening of the tonal colour through playing *sul ponticello*; and on top of this a profusion of dynamic contrasts as a result of which the total sound contradicts all previous musical experience. The shock effect of the first minutes is inescapable; it stamps the piece as a brilliant work of anxiety and oppression from which strange melodies, sounds and rhythms unexpectedly lead us to a realm of unearthly, dream-like truth. If, according to Gottfried Benn's definition, the expressionists began with 'breaking up of language towards the breaking up of the world', then this world here already appears in ruins, but the ruins have become bricks from which a figure as sublime as it is frightening arises.

In May 1947 Schoenberg received from the American Academy of Arts and Letters the one thousand dollar prize for outstanding achievements. His letter thanking them for the honour contains the following highly revealing sentences:

'That you should regard all I have tried to do in the last fifty years as an achievement strikes me as in some respects an overestimate. My own feeling was that I had fallen into an ocean of boiling water; and, as I couldn't swim and knew no other way out, I struggled with my arms and legs as best I could. I don't know what saved me, or why I wasn't drowned or boiled alive—perhaps my own merit was that I never gave in. Whether my movements were very economical or completely senseless, whether they helped or hindered my survival, there was no one willing to help me, and there were plenty who would gladly have seen me go under. I don't think it was envy—what was there to envy?—and I doubt whether it was lack of goodwill, or worse, positive ill-will on their part. Perhaps they just wanted to get rid of the nightmare, the agonising disharmony, the unintelligible thinking, the systematic lunacy that I represented, and I must admit that those who thought in that way were not bad men—though, of course, I could never understand what I had done to them to make them so malicious, so violent and so aggressive. I am still certain that I never took anything from them which was theirs. I never interfered with their rights and privileges, and never trespassed on their preserves. I didn't even know where these lay, or what was the line of demarcation that marked off their estate, or who gave them the right to ownership of the property. I am proud to accept this distinction, awarded on the assumption that I achieved something. Please don't call it false modesty if I say that perhaps something was achieved, but that it is not I who deserves the credit. The credit must go to my opponents. It was they who really helped me.'

There are not many confessions of creative men which surpass this letter in originality. An ocean of boiling water —this is how this man who was never ready to make concessions regarded contact with the world around him. Only a deep, almost religious belief in his own mission could maintain him, and could lend him the strength never to give up. And another thing arises from this confession: the hermetic loneliness he felt surrounding him. This was the subject of his next work. In one stroke, and similarly to the way in which he had written *Erwartung* at the same time of the year, in the late summer, Schoenberg wrote his *Survivor of Warsaw*. By 25 August 1947 the score, for speaker, male chorus and orchestra, was completed. In it experiences are awakened which had lain dormant since the *Ode to Napoleon*. Schoenberg, who in 1938 had identified himself with the Jewish faith in *Kol Nidre*, here becomes the interpreter of an heroic episode in the fight of the Polish Jews against their exterminators. With its shrill dramatic force the work makes an immediate effect. It carries the experience of horror to the listener. In the hours of death of the Warsaw ghetto, the voice of belief is heard, the holy song *Schema Jisroel* against the barbaric noise of the exterminators. The music contains a host of ideas which are difficult to grasp, yet is lapidary in its ever-heightening dynamic effect and its form. It makes a further step in the extension of twelve-note technique.

The *Survivor from Warsaw* was given its first performance in the spring of 1948 at the University of New Mexico by the Albuquerque Orchestra under Kurt Frederick. It was played through twice. At the end of the first performance the listeners remained silent with shock. After the repetition applause, according to the description of an American journalist, thundered through the hall.

In 1947 Schoenberg also completed the manuscript of *Style and Idea*, a book which was published in 1950 by the Philosophical Library of New York, and from which a chapter appeared in a publication of the University of Chicago Press. It is a collection of old and new essays and observations, and is particularly interesting for the numerous examples which Schoenberg includes from his own creative experience.

A number of smaller compositions were written during his last years, including Three Choral Preludes opus 49 on German folk songs of the sixteenth and seventeenth centuries, which Schoenberg contributed to the choral collection of the Arthur Jordan Conservatory in New York. Highly contrapuntal in style, these pieces show Schoenberg's masterly handling of old forms and his intuitive feeling for the style of pre-classical music. Then came the Fantasy for Violin and Piano, only 166 bars long, which Schoenberg wrote for the violinist Adolf Koldofsky who lived in Los Angeles. He played it on Schoenberg's seventy-fifth birthday there for the first time in a concert of the International Society for Contemporary Music. The three songs for low voice and piano opus 48 are earlier. Schoenberg wrote them to poems of Jakob Haringer at the beginning of 1933 in Berlin.

During the years before his death Schoenberg also wrote the two Psalms opus 50a and b, his last completed compositions. The first of the psalms, *Dreimal tausend Jahre* ('Three times a thousand years'), was written in 1949, on a poem of Dagobert C. Runes; the other, *De profundis* of 1950, is a setting of the 130th Psalm in its Hebrew version. Once more these pieces allow a glimpse into a spiritual world where construction and vision penetrate each other in an astonishing manner. *Dreimal tausend Jahre* makes its effect by a hymnlike flatness which is related to the earlier *a cappella* works of the Berlin years. *De profundis* is a compendium of sung and spoken vocal writing in six parts; convulsed everywhere by flashes of intuition, as if threatened by daemonic forces—a last work such as had never been written before.

Schoenberg's enormous literary estate, which was put in order by Josef Rufer only in 1957, contained the manuscript of a theoretical work, *Structional Functions of Harmony*. In Schoenberg's spiritual life, teaching, the transmission of thought to others, had its legitimate place. Every lesson he gave was always a new attempt to simplify the complicated and to deduce the unusual from tradition. From such a double attempt there arose the *Harmonielehre* of 1910, a brilliant, very broadly developed work, typical and indispensable, both in its great knowledge and its small mistakes. What then ran to about five hundred pages, in 1948 was formulated more concisely. Schoenberg's work on this last theoretical book was spread over several years. It is the fruit of a teaching course at the South Californian University of Los Angeles, which Schoenberg started in 1939 and which his assistant Leonard Stein wrote down at the time. Schoenberg completed the manuscript in 1948. Humphrey Searle, the English composer, edited it and published it in London in 1954.

A third of the book (which is two hundred pages long) is no more than a compressed form of the *Harmonielehre*, culminating in a kind of family tree of tonal relationships. The last three chapters examine 'extended tonality', the formal structures of music in their relation to harmony, and finally the situation of modern music—from Mahler, Strauss, Debussy and Reger to Schoenberg, Berg and Webern. Starting from Nietzsche's contrast between the Apollonian and Dionysiac types, Schoenberg here comes to the conclusion that the semi-contrapuntal imitation and the sequential fugato of certain types of modern music can be compared with the old 'Kapellmeister Musik'. As in the *Harmonielehre*, Schoenberg (in agreement with the theories of Debussy) explains dissonances as more distant overtones, i.e. in principle as easy to understand as consonances. According to his definition, the method of composition with twelve notes is the fruit of striving for a deeper logic. Unfortunately this last chapter lacks the music examples that elsewhere so generously illustrate the book. Yet the power to shed light that emanates from this work—as from all of Schoenberg's theoretical writing—is as extraordinary as the daemonic of the music on to whose darkness it sheds its light.

'MOSES UND ARON'

THE AUTHOR of this book travelled through the United States for more than two months in the spring of 1949. Amongst numerous meetings with new and old friends from the Old and New Worlds, those with Arnold Schoenberg were among the most memorable. The last sixteen years had not passed him by without leaving their traces, as in the case of all of us. The lines of that expressive face with the somewhat ironical mouth and the penetrating eyes had become deeper; the features had become sharper and more characteristic. But his stance and his movements were upright and lively as ever, and his wide-awake and rapidly reacting intellect turned every conversation with Schoenberg into an incomparable spiritual adventure. The years had not turned this upright and valiant man into a more conciliatory character. Where he sensed enmity, where he felt an attack on his spiritual and artistic integrity he could not compromise. It is known how sharply he reacted against Thomas Mann when he felt injured by his novel *Doktor Faustus*. This controversy forced many near to both of the disputants to come to painful decisions.

Yet Schoenberg possessed a strong appreciation of and an almost touching gratitude for what he called spiritual faithfulness. Of his friends and pupils many, even the majority, remained faithful to him in this sense. In the conversations with the author in Brentwood Park these, even the ones who had remained in Germany, were frequently mentioned. Schoenberg was even happy at the thought of a summer voyage to Germany, where, during the Darmstadt Holiday

ZWISCHENSPIEL

*)

Tenniket 20/VII.1931

CHOR
(6-stimmig)

Sop.
Mez.
Alt
Tar.
Bs.

Course for Modern Music, he hoped to meet old friends and new admirers. But he did not make the trip, since the doctors felt that it might be too dangerous for his health.

In addition Schoenberg, undeterred by the difficulties his health imposed during the last fifteen years, set himself a further aim. He hoped to complete two big works which were already greatly advanced. They were the oratorio of which the *Jakobsleiter* is the third movement, and the opera *Moses und Aron*. They were works which had been begun long ago, but had been put aside for other tasks. Of the opera two acts were completed; only the third is missing. Schoenberg himself wrote the texts for both works. When the conversation turned on *Moses und Aron*, and the author suggested that the work should be quickly completed, so that it could be performed in Germany, Schoenberg energetically parried the idea. It was not being written with the idea of performances; he even felt that in part it could not be performed at all. Perhaps some time, in the distant future, with synthetic electronic means.

This belief in a Utopian technical progress, coupled with a supreme indifference about having his works performed, is typical of Schoenberg. Both show the same attitude for which Beethoven found the famous words: 'What do I care about this wretched fiddle when the spirit comes over me?' Brahms, when advised to listen to a performance of *Don Giovanni* at the Vienna Opera, declared that he heard the best performance when he read the score.

In the meantime the possibility of performing *Moses und Aron* has twice been proved: in March 1954 the North-West German Radio gave it as a concert performance, and in June 1957 the Stadt-Theater of Zurich staged it, in both cases under the musical direction of Hans Rosbaud, whom Schoenberg had always regarded as one of his most competent interpreters.

The spiritual roots of Schoenberg's big unfinished opera go

deep into the past. At about the time of the first world war Schoenberg wrote texts in which he discussed problems of belief and religion on a philosophical basis. It is in keeping with his character that his intellectual constitution made him a religious man, a believer for whom there existed an eternal order and laws of a higher power. That such a religious approach should not at first have been expressed in a definite religious belief does not detract from its strength. During the years just before the first world war religious and philosophical motifs occupied an increasing part of his thoughts. The text for the oratorio *Die Jakobsleiter* was completed in 1915; in the same year he wrote a text for which no music exists, which has its roots not in religion but in metaphysics, the *Totentanz der Prinzipien*. It is a bizarre poem in monologue in whose penultimate scene a clock in a tower strikes thirteen.

In 1925 Schoenberg wrote an unpublished play, *Der biblische Weg*, and at about this time he began writing the libretto of *Moses und Aron*, thinking of it as a sacred oratorio. The book as we know it today is a poetic creed, a dramatic succession of images which, like the text of the Bible from which it is taken, cannot be measured by a literary yardstick. He treats the intellectual differences of the two brothers, Moses and Aaron, as they appear in the Book of Exodus; Schoenberg's vision ranges from almost literal quotations of the Lutheran text to the daemonic sights of an erotic orgy, a dance of slaughterers, and a blood-sacrifice in which four naked girls are embraced by four priests and are killed with daggers at the moment of highest ecstasy. The scenes of the first act stem from the Bible; the call to Moses from the burning bush, the meeting and conversation of the brothers, the pronouncement of God's word to the people of Israel, the three miracles (the snake, the plague and the changing of water into blood), and the exodus of the people into the wilderness.

The second act is in the main Schoenberg's own invention. It shows Aaron and the people awaiting Moses, who has gone to Sinai to await the giving of the law. To the doubting crowd, Aaron gives the Golden Calf, before which an orgy of drunkenness, madness and sexual licence takes place. After its end Moses returns and there follows the long dramatic discussion between the brothers. Moses, the bearer of the word, has the tables of the law in his hands. He is forced to recognise that Aaron, by orally proclaiming these thoughts, destroys them by making them apparent. Moses even recognises the pillar of fire and the pillar of cloud as forbidden images that detract from the pure image of God. He breaks the tablets of the law; now his thoughts appear to him as madness. With the words, 'O Wort, du Wort, das mir fehlt' ('O Word, thou hast failed me'), he sinks to the ground in despair.

This is as far as Schoenberg's composition goes. The text of the last act consists of a single scene, at the end of which Aaron, the betrayer of thought for the sake of appearance, falls down dead as Moses grants him his freedom. Only a few musical sketches exist for this final act.

With all its wild and brutal details, the text is of Biblical greatness. Schoenberg does not write literature but a creed; the artist has become a prophet. In its description of crude drunkenness the text is related to the pictures of Hell of Hieronymus Bosch; analogies with Paul Claudel can be found in its panoramic breadth and the aesthetic 'indifference' of its drama.

Schoenberg required an unusual orchestra to meet the requirements of a work which combines oratorio with highly dramatic opera. To an enlarged classical orchestra he added piano, harp, celesta, mandolines and a good deal of percussion. The vocalists include six solo singers, a speaker, and both singing and speaking choirs. The style is characterised by frequent combinations of song and rhythmical declamation. Moses is a speaking part, Aaron a lyrical tenor, and it may be taken as symbolic that Moses, the embodiment of thought, is deprived of song.

The glowing orgiastic colours distilled by Schoenberg from the orchestra go far beyond what one knows in his earlier stage works, *Erwartung*, *Glueckliche Hand* and *Von Heute auf Morgen*. One example is the Oriental dance which suddenly begins in the procession around the Golden Calf. Violins and violas strike their open strings *col legno*; the lower strings play harmonics in chords, two mandolines, harp, piano, celesta and xylophone, accompanied by tambourine and triangle, intone rhythmically pliant melody which is later taken up by trombone and piccolo and grows into a remarkably complex polyphony. In sharp contrast is the dance of the slaughterers which follows, with a terrifying huge four-part glissando on three trombones and tuba.

As regards orchestral sound this is unmistakably '*espressivo*' music, with frequent soloistic appearances of individual tonecolours or instrumental solos.

Not less characteristic is Schoenberg's way of using the human voice. Right at the start, when God's voice is heard from the burning bush, he invents for it an imaginative combination of six singing choral soloists and a speaking chorus. The second scene—the big discussion between the brothers Moses and Aaron—musically speaking is a kind of duet for speaking voice and tenor. Recitative, arioso passages, whispering choruses, and antiphonal passages for sung solos and speaking chorus follow one another in ever-changing vocal forms. It is almost beyond human power to register the variety of these phenomena and to grasp them as musical forms. Yet it is impossible to escape from their overwhelming effect.

Each of the singers is characterised by a special style of vocal treatment—the sick woman is a tired, slowly moving contralto, who with her increasing liveliness is taken up to higher registers. The maiden fascinated by the golden god confines herself almost manically to small motivic phrases sung in fast tempo in the soprano register. The Ephraimite has a slow, chromatic circle of ever-returning central notes in the middle range of the baritone compass. The youth has a sharply fluctuating melody striving towards higher and higher regions with a powerful tenor breadth of expression: it is the voice of the idealist and so is sharply differentiated from all the others.

But these are all subsidiary figures. The main singing part which carries the work is that of Aaron; in contrast to Moses, the thinking character who clings to eternity, metaphysics and real values, Aaron is a materialist of everyday life who is impressed by the glitter of gold and the successes of the moment. The part is written for lyrical tenor. Corresponding to Aaron's character, it contains frequent powerful cantilena-like phrases. The chief interval is the fourth, either rising or falling, also frequently reached through the major third, which precedes it like a leading note. The motif of major third and semi-tone accompanies Aaron through the whole opera as well as melodic lines based on broken major and minor triads. Schoenberg observes the principle of transposition of octaves and so increases the number of intervals at his disposal, so that, for example, the semi-tone of Aaron's motif becomes a major seventh; this has its roots in the nature of the *espressivo* style. For the variety of intervals enlarges the means of melodically singable expression and so serves the aim of more perfect interpretation of the action.

Schoenberg always was a genius at the Plus Ultra. He once argued against Goethe's thinking that only when limits are imposed does the master become apparent. His nature, deeply in debt to romanticism, aimed at the infinite. The infinite is the underlying theme of his musical thinking, of his texts and of his religious imagery. Everything he created is filled with the fire of a man who has wrestled with his muse as Jacob wrestled with the angel. The man who as a youngster became a Christian of the Protestant faith, who later returned to the Jewish faith of his fathers, and whose life-work ended with the writing down of thoughts which he called Modern Psalms—this is a man who was spiritually related to the prophets of the Old Testament. The man who revalued all musical values, who felt himself to be a guardian of the highest Western cultural traditions, was a man filled with a Biblical spirit. He once said of himself that he was only the mouthpiece of an idea. This belief in the higher idea for which he lived, in the service of which he acted and created, gave him the strength to pursue his way without compromise to earthly powers or majority demands. He took the things of the spirit more seriously than the majority of his contemporaries, wrestling for the final expression in that language which had been granted him as a musician. If it is the mark of a genius to live for an idea and for a creative force regardless of every opposition from the world around him, then Schoenberg is the essence of the man of genius. *Moses und Aron*, apart from the *Jakobsleiter* which exists only in outline, was his greatest achievement, his legacy and his creed. It had to remain a fragment; but it is a fragment which commands our respect.

DEATH AND LEGACY

Hᴇʀᴍᴀɴɴ Sᴄʜᴇʀᴄʜᴇɴ had already performed part of *Moses und Aron* in the spring of 1951; the Dance round the Golden Calf, the central scene of the second act. The news of the great success of this performance was one of Schoenberg's last pleasures. For months he had been seriously ill. On 13 July, shortly before midnight, his heart ceased to beat. Schoenberg had always feared thirteen as a fateful number for himself.

The months of his last illness had not been without productive work. Schoenberg's thoughts were entirely concentrated on a religious work of art that he called *Modern Psalms*. The literary part of this work, written between 29 September 1950 and 3 July 1951, consists of fifteen poems; a sixteenth was begun. In form the *Modern Psalms* are free verse. Unrhymed, unscanned and without subdivision into verses, and only occasionally heightened in expression, they strike one as the notes of a meditating spirit. They centre around different themes, like prayer (Nos 1 and 13), the granting of prayer, the request to God to punish offenders, the reward of offenders by the devil, the Chosen People (Nos. 5 and 14), in praise of superstition, the miracle as a calculated chess movement by God, the Ten Commandments as a lesson for all peoples, Jesus as the most noble of men, the blessing of love as a friendship of souls and the curse of the love of pleasure, childish belief as a productive contrast to intellectualism, the maintenance of the race through intermarriage. The fragment of the last Psalm ends with the sentence: 'National inbreeding, national incest is as dangerous to the race as to the family and the tribe.'

None of this is high literature; some of it is superficial and should certainly be regarded as no more than a first draft. But it has the power of the spontaneous, of having sprung from a passionate way of thinking. It is philosophical and also theological prose which is meant to be sung. In this, as in several scenes in the *Jakobsleiter* and the opera *Moses und Aron*, lie the inner problems of these texts. They are an acknowledgment of metaphysics, they moralise, they penetrate reality and permit a spiritual world of a higher order to appear in which the symbolism of numbers, the theory of probabilities and the cybernetics of computers take their place beside the mechanism of reason. The fifteenth Psalm is an extensive criticism of the orthodox as well as the liberal Jew, but ends with the statement that only strict Judaism could save the world from a Sodom and Gomorrah and lead it to the 'paradise-like balanced contentment' which is also praised in the tenth Psalm.

Only with the first of these texts was Schoenberg able to show what he hoped to realise musically. The short score, which breaks off after bar 85, was written out by Rudolf Kolisch as a full score. Completely in the sense of the Old Testament Psalms, the poem is a dialogue with God, a piece of philosophical lyricism that deals with the nature and purpose of prayer. Schoenberg opposes the 'I' to the Jewish God, 'the only, eternal, all-powerful, all-knowing and unimaginable, of whom I neither can nor must make an image'. In his text for the *Jakobsleiter* he had quoted from Balzac's *Seraphita*: 'He who prays has become one with God'. The text of the first Modern Psalm too is based on this unity with God, for it concludes with 'And yet I pray, for I do not desire to lose the blessed feeling of unity, of communication with Thee.'

With the words 'And yet I pray' the composition ends, and the work sounds like a last call to God from the man who, like Gabriel in the *Jakobsleiter*, wished to change mankind. The short fragment is related in a worthy manner to the religious compositions of the later period in California, the *Kol Nidre* and the two unaccompanied choruses opus 50a and b. To a five-part mixed chorus Schoenberg adds a speaker and a small orchestra consisting of flute, oboe, cor anglais, two clarinets, bass clarinet, bassoon, horn, trumpet, trombone and string quartet. The speaker, who carries the main task of interpreting the text, has a part which is notated in the manner used since *Pierrot Lunaire*, with the exact rhythm and the quasi-melodic rise and fall of the Sprechgesang.

Schoenberg avoids any suggestion of psalmody, and builds the composition in the style of dramatically heightened expressiveness that characterises all of his music. The Psalm is not tonal, but is written in a manner similar to that used for the seven-year-older *Ode to Napoleon* in its masterly use of twelve-note technique. Also the row out of which the composition is developed is similar to that of the *Ode*. It consists of two groups of six notes, the second half being identical with the retrograde mirror form of the first half transposed down one tone: E-D sharp-C-A flat-B-G—F-A-F sharp-B flat-C sharp-D. In addition the inversion of the first half has a similar relation to the second half of the basic row. From this, analogies arise which provide an even closer unity of melodic line than can usually be found in dodecaphonic works with normal rows. Finally the row contains in itself triadic groups in close position which are sometimes used bitonally, as in the fifth to the eighth bars, where A flat major and E minor are combined in parallel.

The structure is highly contrapuntal; from the choral beginning where E and D sharp, alternating as minor ninths and major sevenths, grate against each other, the voices develop to ever-increasing independence. Imitative passages like the 'Who am I' sung fortissimo and the mirror canon of the chorus and orchestra to the words 'When I tell God' are the clearest characteristics of this kind of polyphonic thinking, here used to serve the meaning of the words. Dynamically the Psalm has great variety. The first entry of the women's voices at 'Oh Thou my God' is *forte*, accompanied *pianissimo* by the wind instruments after a short *forte* accent. The strength of sound then quickly decreases to *piano*, to be driven suddenly up to *fortissimo* at 'Who am I'. The first climax is the great unison of the woodwind and the high strings at the spoken words 'He who will grant my passionate prayer or not consider it'. The tone-colour is as varied as the dynamic picture. Schoenberg makes accents of colour with a gripping, sometimes frightening strength. The contrasts of spoken words, words sung by the chorus and orchestral polyphony are curiously contrasted with the relative simplicity of the passages which are confined to only six-note material for long stretches.

In this last compositional fragment from Schoenberg's hand can be found all the intellectual force and vision that made his music the magnetic pole of an epoch. Those who study the score and the Psalm texts published in facsimile will recognise that here an individual found himself at one with his God. The striving after God and Schoenberg's religiosity are thus revealed as a phenomenon as important as the mystique of numbers which exerts the same pull in his music as in the Masses of the devout Netherlands polyphonists and in the fugues of Bach.

The effect of Schoenberg's music is, like every true creative process, independent of its material diffusion. The more conductors and interpreters refuse to perform his work, the more irresistible the spirit of his works becomes. Even the attempt to declare atonal music as biologically inferior, as was recently done,[1] does not alter the fact that it is a legitimate form of art in the twentieth century.

[1] Furtwängler, *Gespräche über Musik* (Zürich 1948).

In particular, the years since the second world war have shown how convincingly Schoenberg's ideas of a new order of sound material appeal to the younger generation. In Paris the school of the dodecaphonists, under the leadership of René Leibowitz, has become a feared spiritual power. In Italy Luigi Dallapiccola has made twelve-note music his own. At the congress of the dodecaphonists which took place in Milan in May 1949 composers and theoreticians of many countries were represented. In England and Norway, in Germany and Switzerland, in Brazil and the United States the new technique is not only practised but also taught in colleges of music.

It would be wrong to demand that kind of totality for it which some of its most radical young proponents have done. Schoenberg himself warned his disciples against orthodoxy. Long ago his eternally searching spirit had left behind the first steps of a one-sided dogmatism which had to be followed in the early years of the development of the new technique.

Already in 1925, in an essay *Gesinnung oder Erkenntnis* (Jahrbuch der Universal-Edition 1926), to the question whether it was right to write tonally or atonally, or whether the one or the other was even necessary or impossible, he had given the most thoughtful reply: 'He who can do a thing cleanly will be able to do it either tonally or atonally.'

Schoenberg is the brilliant scientist of compositional technique, the pursuer regardless and undivertible of the path which he characterised as the German-Austrian music tradition *par excellence*. The liquidation of tonality, the emancipation of the dissonance through the according of equal values to all possible sounds—that is his work. That he reached his goal, not by a theoretical path but through the force of an inner compulsion, his development unequivocally proves. What his style has made possible in the ways of new possibilities of musical expression, chords built up of fourths, the technique of 'wandering' leading notes, irregular rhythms free from the bar-line, melody in huge leaps and 'unmelodic' steps, linear polyphony and the splitting up of the development section taken over from sonata-form—all this is already history today and has gone over into the language of almost all important composers.

The real problem, though, of Schoenberg's music is to be found in its curious inner dualism. The most differentiated feeling for 'in-between' values in sound is most oddly linked in it with abstract intellectuality. While Schoenberg the compositorial process of creation seemingly keeps strictly to the immanent laws of sound material and its dialectical development, the sound experience appeals incessantly to the most hidden layers of the aesthetic subconscious. His music—whose completely spontaneous origin is vouched for by a thousand examples—uncovers inner associations even in its most complicated and apparently most cerebral forms, as a side-product, so to speak; only depth-psychology or—to take a literary parallel—the lyricism of Rilke's *Duino Elegies*, or the prose of Marcel Proust and James Joyce—have done this in such a stirring and disquieting way.

Such 'depth effects' almost preclude 'easy', playful or naïvely light-hearted emotions. The somnambulistic character of these works of art is illuminated by the stars of fear, oppression, of sudden knowledge and death. Thus Schoenberg's music is in no way 'happy music-making' or 'musicianly' and it is also foreign to the motor *ostinato* rhythm of the Stravinsky school. It contains few repetitions; what has been said once does not appear worth saying again except in a varied form.

Stravinsky himself has changed in his spiritual relation to Schoenberg since about 1948. He was so strongly impressed in 1912 by the instrumentation of *Pierrot Lunaire* that some of his works which he wrote immediately afterwards, above all the *Trois poésies de la lyrique japonaise*, clearly showed Schoenberg's influence. Later the two chief masters of modern music were to take ever more divergent paths: soon after 1920 Schoenberg's twelve-note technique and Stravinsky's neo-classicism became the guiding lines for two separate and apparently irreconcilable branches of music.

Yet with the Mass of 1947 Stravinsky began to use contrapuntal methods which brought him closer to Schoenberg. With the Septet, the Cantata, the canonic *In Memoriam Dylan Thomas* and the Shakespeare songs he adopted the technique of serial composition, at first with rows of only five to eight notes. Finally, in the *Canticum Sacrum*, performed for the first time in Venice in 1956, two movements are built on a twelve-note row, worked with the typical technique of the Schoenbergian school. Since then Stravinsky has repeatedly expressed his admiration for this school, in particular for the works of Anton Webern. Thus the gap was bridged that for decades had separated the leading spirits of modern music. Schoenberg himself, who did not live to see this development, also found words of praise in the last years of his life for Stravinsky, and took his side in one concrete case of a sharp philosophical attack directed against the Russian master.

The further Schoenberg's very personal style developed, the more strongly the absolutism of his music appeared. Even where the marriage of word and sound belongs to the nature of the work, in songs and in choruses, in melodrama and in operas (i.e. in half of Schoenberg's works), the text determines the character but never the form of its music. The witness of this is the composer who has projected Schoenberg's example most brilliantly to the outside world—Alban Berg in his operas *Wozzeck* and *Lulu*. The aesthetic absolutism of Schoenberg goes so far that he even refuses the smallest demands of nonmusical forces in music, whether they stem from literature, theatre, film, technique or even practical music making.

If today one likes to reject Schoenberg as an over-intellectual esoteric, and if, perhaps on the basis of the Russian thesis of socialist realism, one opposes to him a new type of emotional music, this is the same kind of objection which, about 1750, a new generation raised against the old Bach. The uncompromising single-mindedness with which Schoenberg proceeded must however gain him respect and reverence even in those quarters where people do not wish to follow him. As a personality, as a pioneer, he is indeed more exposed to scorn and defamation than any other of his contemporaries. Yet his figure, his teaching and his example are a permanent feature of our time.

WORKS BY ARNOLD SCHOENBERG

OPUS	TITLE	DATE OF COMPOSITION	PUBLISHER
1	Two songs for baritone and piano	1896–8	Birnbach, Berlin
2	Four songs with piano	1896–8	Birnbach, Berlin
3	Six songs with piano	1896–8	Birnbach, Berlin
4	*Verklärte Nacht*, for string sextet	1899	Birnbach, Berlin
	Version for string orchestra	1917	Universal
	Revised version of above	1943	Universal
—	*Gurrelieder*, for soloists, chorus and orchestra	1900–1	Universal
	Orchestration completed	1911	
5	*Pelleas und Melisande*, symphonic poem	1902–3	Universal
6	Eight songs for voice and piano	1905	Birnbach
7	String Quartet No. 1 in D minor	1904–5	Birnbach
8	Six songs for voice and orchestra	1903–4	Universal
9	Chamber Symphony No. 1 in E major	1906	Universal
9b	Version of above with strings doubled		
10	String Quartet No. 2 in F sharp minor with soprano voice	1907–8	Universal
11	Three piano pieces	1908	Universal
12	Two ballads for voice and piano	1906	Universal
13	*Friede auf Erden*, for *a cappella* chorus	1907	Schott
14	Two songs for voice and piano	1907	Universal
15	Fifteen songs for voice and piano on poems of Stefan George (Das Buch der Hängenden Gärten)	1908	Universal
16	Five pieces for orchestra	1909	Peters
17	*Erwartung*, monodrama for mezzo-soprano and orchestra	1909	Universal
18	*Die glückliche Hand*, drama with music	1909–13	Universal
19	Six little piano pieces	1911	Universal
20	*Herzgewächse*, for soprano, celesta, harmonium and harp	1911	Universal

OPUS	TITLE	DATE OF COMPOSITION	PUBLISHER
21	*Pierrot Lunaire*, for speaker and five instrumentalists	1912	Universal
22	Four songs with orchestra	1913–15	Universal
23	Five piano pieces	1923	Hansen, Copenhagen
24	Serenade for seven instruments and bass voice	1923	Hansen
25	Suite for piano	1924	Universal
26	Wind Quintet	1924	Universal
27	Four pieces for mixed chorus	1925	Universal
28	Three Satires for mixed chorus	1925	Universal
29	Suite for seven instruments	1927	Universal
30	String Quartet No. 3	1926	Universal
31	Variations for orchestra	1927–8	Universal
32	*Von Heute auf Morgen*, opera in one act	1929	Schott
33a	Piano piece	1932	Universal
33b	Piano piece	1932	New Music, San Francisco
34	Accompaniment Music for a Film Scene, for orchestra	1930	Heinrichshofen, Magdeburg
35	Six pieces for male chorus *a cappella*	1930	Bote and Bock
—	Suite for strings in G major	1934	Schirmer
36	Violin Concerto	1936	Schirmer
37	String Quartet No. 4	1937	Schirmer
38	Chamber Symphony No. 2	1906–40	Schirmer
38b	Version of above for piano duet		
39	*Kol Nidre*, for speaker, chorus and orchestra	1938	Schirmer
40	Variations on a Recitative, for organ	1943	Gray, New York
41	*Ode to Napoleon Bonaparte*, for speaker, string quartet and piano	1942	Schirmer
41b	Version of above with string orchestra	1943	
42	Piano Concerto	1942	Schirmer
43	Theme and Variations for wind orchestra	1943	Schirmer
43b	Version of above for full orchestra		
—	Two three-part canons	1943	Musical Quarterly, New York
44	*Prelude to a Genesis Suite*, for orchestra and chorus	1945	

OPUS	TITLE	DATE OF COMPOSITION	PUBLISHER
45	String Trio	1946	Bomart, New York
46	*A Survivor from Warsaw*, for speaker, chorus and orchestra	1947	Bomart
47	Fantasy for violin and piano	1949	Peters
48	Three songs for low voice and piano	1933	Bomart
49	Three German folk songs for *a cappella* chorus		Marks
50a	*Dreimal tausend Jahre*, for mixed *a cappella* chorus	1950	Israel Music Publications
50b	*De Profundis*, for six-part chorus	1950	Israel Music Publications

UNFINISHED WORKS

—	*Die Jakobsleiter*, oratorio	1913–	
—	*Moses und Aron*, opera	1931–	Schott
50c	*Modern Psalm*, for speaker, chorus and orchestra	1950–	Schott

INDEX

Altenberg, Peter, 31
Antheil, George, 105
Apostel, H. E., 114
Armitage, Merle, 116

Bach, D. J., 18, 114
Bach, J. S., 51, 59, 76, 82, 85, 86, 103, 110, 156, 160
Bahr, Hermann, 31
Balzac, 154
Bartók, 34, 42, 118
Beardsley, Aubrey, 66
Beethoven, 25, 37, 45, 72, 76, 83, 119
Bekker, Paul, 55, 91
Benda, Georg, 62
Benn, Gottfried, 136, 139
Berg, Alban, 13, 33-4, 50, 56, 78, 79, 86, 91, 96, 97, 114, 116, 143, 159
Bethge, Hans, 97-8
Blitzstein, Marc, 96
Blonda, Max, 103
Bosch, Hieronymus, 149
Brahms, 18, 19, 20, 25, 29, 32, 51, 59, 76, 101, 127, 128, 129, 147
Braque, Georges, 47
Bruch, Max, 120
Bruckner, 19, 32
Buck, Pearl S., 112
Buhlig, Richard, 73
Bülow, Hans von, 73
Busoni, 49-50, 57, 64, 73, 91, 93
Byron, 124

Casella, Alfredo, 91, 118
Castelnuovo-Tedesco, Mario, 131
Chopin, 23
Claudel, Paul, 149
Coolidge, Elizabeth Sprague, 101, 117, 118
Cowell, Henry, 96

Dallapiccola, Luigi, 157
Debussy, 22, 23, 24, 28-9, 42, 47, 52, 78, 82, 143, 144
Dehmel, Richard, 23, 24, 26, 37
Deutsch, Max, 76

Deutsch, Moritz, 120
Diaghilev, 65
Dowson, Ernest, 72

Einstein, 132
Eisler, Hanns, 76, 91
Engel, Carl, 129
Essberger, Karl, 61

Fitzner Quartet, 20
Frederick, Kurt, 141
Freud, Siegmund, 31, 134
Freund, Marya, 91
Fried, Oskar, 57
Fries, H. W. de, 61
Furtwängler, Wilhelm, 92, 102, 156n.

George, Stefan, 42-3, 45, 46, 47, 72
Gerhard, Roberto, 95
Gershwin, George, 116-7
Giraud, Albert, 21, 60, 62, 64-7, 69
Gluck, 62
Goehr, Rudolf, 96
Goehr, Walter, 95, 96
Goethe, 36, 151
Golyscheff, Jefim, 83
Graf, Dr Herbert, 104
Gravina, Count Gilbert, 73
Gray, Allan, 95
Greissle, Felix, 22, 80
Gronostay, Walter, 95
Gropius, Manon, 97n.
Gutheil-Schoder, Marie, 44, 79, 91

Hába, Alois, 114
Handel, 59, 76, 111, 113, 135
Hannenheim, Norbert von, 96
Hanslick, Eduard, 19, 32
Harrell, Mack, 125
Harrison, Lou, 130
Hart, Julius, 37
Hartleben, Otto Erich, 21, 60, 62, 65-7, 71
Hauer, Josef Mathias, 13, 83, 85, 86, 99
Hauptmann, Gerhard, 37
Hausegger, Siegmund von, 36
Haydn, 43, 76